RUBBLE FLORA

THE
SEAGULL
LIBRARY OF
GERMAN
LITERATURE

Volker Braun

RUBBLE FLORA

SELECTED POEMS

Translated by
David Constantine and Karen Leeder

LONDON NEW YORK CALCUTTA

This publication was supported by a grant
from the Goethe-Institut India

Seagull Books, 2019

ISBN 978 0 8574 2 714 4

British Library Cataloguing-in-Publication Data
A catalogue record for this book is available from the British Library

Typeset by Seagull Books, Calcutta, India
Printed and bound by WordsWorth India, New Delhi, India

CONTENTS

From *Dances of Death*

3
Findings

ACKNOWLEDGEMENTS

Some of these poems, or earlier versions of them, have appeared in *MPT*, *International Poetry Review*, *Poetry Review* and *Kalendergeschichten* (Goethe-Institut, 2012).

Thanks go to Petra Hardt at Suhrkamp and to Seagull Books for taking on the volume, but especially to Volker Braun for his support and his patient answers to the many questions; and to Volker and Anneli for hospitality and friendship.

David Constantine and Karen Leeder

Volker Braun is one of Germany's foremost lyric poets. First in the German Democratic Republic (or former East Germany), where he began his literary career, and after 1990 in the Berlin Republic, he has published some ten volumes of poetry and received numerous major awards for his writing, including the Bremer Literature Prize (1986) the Schiller Memorial Prize (1992), the German Critics' Prize (1996) the Erwin Strittmatter Prize (1998) and the prestigious Georg Büchner Prize (2000) awarded by the German Academy for Language and Literature. Recent years have brought international honours, including the Candide Prize (2009) and appointment as Chevalier in the 'Ordre des Arts et des Lettres' (2012). From 1999 to 2000 he was the Brother Grimm Professor at the University of Kassel and he served as the Director of the Literature Section of the German Academy of Arts (2006–10). He began as a poet, and it is arguably his poetry that will be his most distinctive and long-lasting legacy. But he is perhaps better known, internationally at least, as a dramatist, novelist and essayist. His plays are frequently performed in Germany and beyond; his controversial *Unvollendete Geschichte* (1975, published 1988), or his *Hinze-Kunze Roman* of 1985, following the adventures of a party hack and his chauffeur, remain blistering insights into power relations within the socialist state. Equally, since 1990, his picaresque exposure of the inadequacy and indignity of welfare reform and back-to-work programmes, *Machwerk*

(2008), and particularly a number of shorter, darkly satirical narrative pieces have carved out for him a central place in contemporary German literature. Nevertheless, all Braun's texts are linked: drama, essays, novels and poetry all borrow from one another and form an organic whole that is bound up with his life. Braun is a political poet—in that from the beginning, his work has been filled with rage, grief and a determined hope in the face of history in the making. But his poetry has also always transcended national and political borders, seeking out the possibilities of being human in poems that insist on the love, humour and beauty of our lives and the solace of the natural world.

Braun was born in Dresden on 7 May 1939 as one of five brothers. His father fell in the last days of the War and his sixth birthday was the day of liberation and Allied (in his case, Soviet) occupation. His childhood was spent in the ruins of Dresden, and the 'rubble flora' that gave the title to one of his early poems (and to this volume) was at once the vegetation growing on the ruined German landscape after the Second World War and the flowering of a new society after the fall of fascism. As a political non- conformist, however, Braun was often at odds with the regime. Initially refused entry to university for political reasons, like many young writers, he spent time in industry; working in a printing firm, in civil engineering and in mining before he could take up philosophy studies in Leipzig (1960–64). He came to prominence as one of a new generation of poets in the 1960s; a group that included Wolf Biermann, Günter Kunert, Sarah and Rainer Kirsch, Karl Mickel and Heinz Czechowski. Several of these writers also hailed from the same province of Saxony (that is such a vivid presence in Braun's poetry) and, having studied under the tutelage of the great poet Georg Maurer at the Johannes

R. Becher Literary Institute in Leipzig, became known along with others as the 'Saxon School of Poets' on account of their shared references, themes and their commitment to the distinctive landscape and its dialects.

Braun's first collection of poetry, tellingly entitled *Provokation für mich*, was presented to the Academy of Arts by an older mentor, poet Stephan Hermlin, in 1962 and almost led to Braun being exmatriculated. The collection rings with the pioneering spirit of the young East German state and scorns complacency and stasis. 'Don't come to us with it all sewn up. We need work in progress' is the first line of the famous poem 'Demand'. Braun's rallying cry summons the young out of their arm chairs to work towards the collective goal. But this was very different from the familiar agit-prop, as the authorities were quick to notice. The young Braun had learnt from Walt Whitman, Friedrich Hölderlin, Pablo Neruda, Vladimir Mayakowsky and, above all, critical socialist icon Bertolt Brecht. Enthusiasm is constantly debunked with irony; elevated tones with flippant asides; long rangy lines and exclamations rub shoulders with sober observation. For Braun, anything directive, operative or definitive is overturned in favour of the transitional, self-questioning and unstable. But in the early 1960s, at the height of political tensions with the West, the GDR authorities were determined to defend really existing socialism as the best of all possible worlds, and Braun's was a provocation too far.

He was offered a haven of sorts by Brecht's widow Helene Weigel, who invited him to take up the role of artistic director in Brecht's theatre, the Berliner Ensemble. But there was no real hiding place in the GDR and Braun's first play was immediately banned and could only be performed a decade later under a new title. The same fate befell his next play,

Lenins Tod, in which the revolutionary leader recognizes the disaster of the revolution. This only saw the light of day 18 years after completion. A course was set that would define Braun's relationship with authority throughout his time in the GDR—the need to find a way of writing that would reach his readers, but also evade the censor. Put negatively, this is the 'slave language' characteristic of art in a dictatorship. But viewed in another light, it accounts for the sense when reading Braun's poetry that the language is constantly under enormous pressure and that much of the meaning stems from what is not said, from a kind of shadow dialectic operating under the surface.

After the events of the Prague Spring, like many fellow artists and writers, Braun became gradually more open in his criticism of life in socialism and more sceptical about the possibility of reform. But it was the enforced expatriation in 1976 of one of Braun's fellow poets, the stridently critical singer-songwriter Wolf Biermann, that changed everything. For Braun, as for many of his contemporaries, this act of brute Realpolitik demonstrated once and for all that the paranoid and controlling mechanisms of the state could not be trusted to deliver the progress towards a truly humane society that had been so long promised. Braun was one of the first to sign a petition against the action and his unwillingness to withdraw his signature, despite pressure from above, brought him under permanent surveillance from the Stasi, or East German secret police. This perhaps explains the darkening of his work, along with the sense of threat expressed in a poem like 'Fief' (1980): 'I'll hold out here, find succour in the East, / Spouting stuff that one fine day could cost / Me my neck. I'm still standing at my post.'

Braun was successful in publishing critiques of the socialist state, even though he was a member of the East German Communist Party, on account of his ability to manoeuvre within the system. A communist who mistrusted communism; a writer who wanted to play a part in the great movement of history, but at every turn felt himself bound and restricted: 'Every step I've still to take, / tears me apart.' For a time he was able to publish successfully in the East (and simultaneously in the West with the prestigious Suhrkamp Verlag) and win some of the major prizes that his country had to offer, while constantly testing and stretching the boundaries of what could be said. But this was not possible without compromise—as documented in the tortuous censorship history of any number of his works. And the poem 'Fief' concludes bitterly: 'The fief I need is not awarded as a prize.' Whatever the genre—poetry, drama, novels or stories—Braun's ability to survive was dependent on his knack for maintaining a political and existential balancing act. At what cost, however, becomes clear in his caustic 1993 poem 'Balance'.

That the same option was not possible for many of his contemporaries is demonstrated by the (often enforced) exodus of writers to the West during the late 1970s. Braun's 1977 poem 'Der Müggelsee', named after a lake in the suburbs of East Berlin (and not included in this selection), records the growing feeling of isolation as the friends who had once 'sat in the same boat' depart one by one. Equally, for many of the younger writers arriving on the poetry scene at that time, there was never an option of inclusion, let alone publication. They lived instead a precarious, quasi-illegal underground existence and viewed Braun's negotiations with power with frank incomprehension. However, after working in Leipzig for a spell, then at the Deutsches Theater in Berlin before returning to the Berliner Ensemble, all the while battling with the censors at every turn, Braun left the Writers' Union of East Germany in 1982.

His collection of 1987, *Langsamer knirschender Morgen*, first published in West Germany, tells the unambiguous story of a state in terminal decline. The 'iron times' that Braun's friend Karl Mickel spoke of in 1975 inspired Braun's image of the 'iron truck' of progress that has come to a halt—life is at a stand-still, everything exists in a limbo of devastated hopes. Images of existential winter abound in a blasted landscape. His poetry goes in search of another reality; and this is the world of an 'innermost Africa' (the title of one of the poems) lit by a transgressive and emancipatory longing. Braun's influential essay of 1984, 'Rimbaud. Ein Psalm der Aktualität', celebrates his affinity with the French modernist poet, especially the Rimbaud of the visionary 'Illuminations', and at the same time sets out a radical aesthetic and existential programme which finds expression in his poems—an exuberant 'freeing of the senses'. Snippets of quotation are spliced together to form a journey that is intensely lyrical but also fractured and open-ended. This project is driven by what Braun had called in the poem 'Definition' of 1975 'the search for the stuff (of writing, of living)' and gives rise to Braun's 'material poems', a sporadic sequence spread over a number of collections, which were gathered into perhaps his most accomplished and outspoken volume of verse in 1990, *Der Stoff zum Leben 1–3*, the title of which might be rendered 'Material for Living' or perhaps 'The Stuff of Life'—later republished and expanded to four sections.

The word 'Stoff', meaning material or stuff, is at once 'such stuff as dreams are made on', as signalled by the overt debt to Shakespeare in the collection, but also the reality of dialectical materialism and, finally, the concrete material of the poem. These are long, tentative texts searching out and simultaneously commenting on their own processes as they go—picking up and responding to fragments of Goethe, Lessing, Che Guevara, Benjamin, Hölderlin or Whitman. A case in point is the poem 'Walter Benjamin in the Pyrenees', which tracks the Jewish philosopher's flight from the Nazis across the precarious mountain pass towards Spain and his suicide but also constructs the poem itself: 'Step by step, as chance / Offers a narrow foothold / In the material'. But these poems also highlight Braun's growing anxiety about ecological themes—literally the stuff of life is running out. And the daring inclusion of a motto from T. S. Eliot's *Waste Land*, which leads to the pointed question 'Shall I at least set my lands in order?', indicates the multiple levels at which the volume operates.

It is these years perhaps that cement Braun's distinctive and immediately recognizable sound and have earned him the reputation as one of the outstanding writers of our times. Whatever the form, his work worries at the question of political and personal emancipation: 'How long will the earth endure us / And what shall we call freedom'—lines that conclude his poem 'After the Massacre of Illusions' and reappear in his Büchner Prize acceptance speech of 2000. He criticized the failures of 'really existing socialism', was spied on and censored by the state, but never turned his back on his country, nor gave up hope that one day—also by means of literature—things could be changed for the better. His poetry identifies with that possibility, 'the Principle of Hope' inspired by the Marxist philosopher Ernst Bloch, but is given its devastating traction by the fact that the possibility never became reality. And that discrepancy is not described from the outside but expressed from within. Multiple voices, rhetorical figures and existential attitudes are spliced together. Political jargon or quotations from fellow poets appear in upper case or italics or, more often than not, unidentified in the poems. Major events of history and personal biography are woven together. Lines are fractured, chased across the page. Punctuation is sparing, allowing clauses to be released from their semantic context and become grammatically unstable, thus putting the reader constantly on the back foot. The literary principle of his work lies precisely in the friction, the rubbing up the wrong way of all these different idioms and meanings, whether in free form, collage, blocks of prose, sonnets or classical verse. This makes for difficult poems perhaps, at odds with the mainstream of Anglo-Saxon poetry, but as Braun explains in his essays, his fractured aesthetic reflects the fractured times.

The distillation and dialectical thinking learnt under censorship would come to serve him well after the fall of the Berlin Wall. Braun was one of those who supported a 'third way' of reform socialism and the keeping of an independent, democratic East Germany in opposition to what he saw as the debased vales of the West. He was one of the signatories of the resolution 'For our Country', famously proclaimed by leading intellectuals on Berlin's Alexanderplatz in November 1989. But even before the euphoria had died down, it had been overtaken by history. The revolutionary slogan 'Wir sind das Volk' (we are the people) had morphed into 'Wir sind *ein* Volk' (we are *one* people), and what many on the left saw as the annexation of the former East Germany and the surrender of its identity and ideals was already underway.

It was Braun's poem 'Property', published simultaneously in a number of national newspapers in 1990 (under its original title 'Obituary') that crystallized the historical moment and became perhaps the most famous document of those times. With a mixture of bitterness and despair, it set out what had been truly lost: 'What I never owned, they've taken even this. / What I never lived, I know I'll always miss'. The form of the poem and a number of images in it indicate that it has been conceived as a direct response to the earlier poem 'Fief' of 1980. The 'property' it mourns is not simply the obliteration of the collective ownership of the workers' state, nor its unrealized ideals. It is the loss of the place of the poet. At the centre of the poem comes the bald assertion: 'I don't know the meaning of my text'. But the first title, 'Obituary', is also significant—from this point many of Braun's poems come to inhabit a no-man's land marked by death.

Thus if the first section of our collection, 'Prussia, Pleasure Garden' charts Braun's response to life under German communism, the second, 'The Massacre of Illusions', takes up in 1990 and offers Braun's searing vision of triumphant capitalism and its victims. Far from an era in transition or the beginning of a new and better future, Braun sees it as an end time. His short collection of 1999, *Tumulus*, confirms this impression. The Latin title (meaning 'sepulchral mound') suggests a position and an aesthetic literally founded on death—the loss or 'burial' of political illusions in the German Democratic Republic and the Federal Republic as well. Now the 'material' of the poems, as Braun himself commented in an interview that same year—'is fetched up out of the graves. If something new is to come something must go.' But what is it that has gone and what has come in its place? Braun offers a brutal answer: 'Socialism's out the door, but here comes Johnnie Walker' ('O Chicago! O Contradiction!'). This is not that crude nostalgia for the East that brought a new word into the German language—'Ostalgie'. The poems make no bones about the corrupt degeneracy of really existing socialism, but nor are they in thrall to the 'barbaric beauty' of really existing capitalism. The result is a state of existential placelessness marked with sorrow—the lyric subject finds himself time and again 'A nomad in the four-star hotel / . . . the throw-away man' ('The Magma in the Heart of the Tuareg'), or mourning his and the era's failures at the bedside of his dying mother in the moving '6. 5. 1996'. It would be wrong to see this as simply a poetry of despair, however. Braun, as a number of his other contemporaries, notably the great dramatist and poet Heiner Müller, projects the collapse of the GDR and the triumph of capitalism onto the backdrop of the downfall of ancient Rome and the rise of the Roman Empire. In increasingly classicizing metres and tightening forms, Braun bears witness to an endgame on a grand scale but also to the satirical possibilities of the new global context. 'The Empire Considers a Map of the World' of 2003, for example, will debunk the grotesque posturing of the USA and its coalition of the willing as the new world order takes hold. There is bitterness here; but Braun has learnt to blend frustration with irony and equanimity with continuing social outrage.

The poems gathered in our final section, 'Findings', are taken from Braun's 2005 collection, *An die schönen Possen*, and other, uncollected, poems up to 2013. They continue the themes of the earlier work and are self-consciously 'late' poems that are marked by an intensely lyric vulnerability. Reflections on mortality and physical frailty (weakening eyes, for example) and variations on personal and epochal failure make for a mood of melancholy contemplation. And yet what gives the collection its bite is its insistence on the celebration of the human in spite of, or because of, that vulnerability. The title of the collection refers to Sir Philip Sidney's rejection of the earthly in a poem of old age: 'Leave me, O Love, which reaches but to dust, / And thou, my mind, aspire to higher things'. Braun's determined rebuttal spurns any thoughts of higher things in favour of the joys and appetites of the here and now. An example is the remarkable cycle, 'Dances of Death', where the ideals of the past are grotesquely morphed into a modern recasting of the mediaeval 'danse macabre' across the detritus, starvation, and plummeting share-prices of contemporary capitalism. The hopes of one age have become the down-and-outs of another. But these poems are counterbalanced by poems of love and sex as intimations of the truly human and the anger is in turn curtailed by a drastic humour and a more wistful calm: 'A vale of joys, / This life of ours' ('Tides').

Here, and in his more recent uncollected poems, Braun's gaze falls on contemporary society with an acuity scarcely less blistering than in GDR days. The entry to the twenty-first century is greeted with scepticism '—From a short // Century into a meaningless one'; society is presented as a pilotless plane careering towards oblivion with its cargo of 'premium trash in economy class' concerned only with 'shopping and fucking' ('Shakespeare Shuttle'). Poems document the disastrous realities of our world—from the attack on the World Trade Centre in September 2001, to the Iraq war, the financial crash, the notorious Hartz IV welfare reforms in Germany, the indiscriminate slaughter on the Norwegian island of Utøya, or the brutal suppression of demonstrations on Istanbul's Taksim Square in 2013. One of the key poems of this period is 'Cashing Up' (2000\9). It is the third in Braun's series of core poems that take the temperature of the historical moment, along with 'Fief' (1980) and 'Property' (1990). In a world where people's lives are at the mercy of the market, where they sell 'blood, soul and tears' for the minimum wage, Braun asks 'What have we become, what can we be?' The diagnosis is blunt: 'A race of beggars. Insult to my injury'.

And yet the poems are not unremittingly bleak. In his acceptance speech on receiving the Büchner Prize, Braun had commented: 'We know bestiality . . . but hardly know humanity any longer. When the ideas are buried, out come the bones' (words that reappear in his poem 'After the Massacre of Illusions'). The search for the shrinking places in a contemporary world where the human can thrive becomes an urgent concern of the late poems. In his poem to Parsley Island, the tiny uninhabited lump of rock in the Strait of Gibraltar that provoked a brief territorial war between Spain and Morocco in 2002, the contested fleck of white on the map, the 'ownerless coast', offers a (short-lived) utopian promise. The theme is continued in 'Das unbesetze Gebiet' of 2004, a prose piece about the strange fate of the area of Schwarzenberg in the Erzgebirge region of Germany that existed for 42 days in 1945 belonging to no one and became a kind of anachronistic hope. And it is the flowering of this frail possibility against the odds that Braun's recent poetry seeks and celebrates wherever he may find it—in the collapse of the 'citadels of finance' ('Iguanas'), in the 'wilderness' (the 10-part sequence of 2012, inspired by Ezra Pound, which will surely become one of Braun's most important works), in the thick of 'twitter storms', or the elemental rubble of the universe. In this he is, perhaps, not so very far from his beginnings—'rubble flora' indeed.

The following selection of poems, arranged broadly chronologically, takes its lead from the hugely influential, if idiosyncratic, *Selected Poems* chosen by Braun and issued by Suhrkamp in 1996: *Lustgarten, Preußen*. The first section of that volume, though covering the longest span (1959–74) was also the shortest and most selective, eschewing some of the most famous of the early demonstrative poems. Similarly, many of the long poems of the middle phase were absent— 'West Shore', which Braun considers the centre of his oeuvre—being a notable exception. The final section, just over a quarter of the volume, covered just seven years (1988–95), marking Braun's bitter reckoning with collapse of his homeland and the Berlin Republic. Much of that general shape has been preserved here, though in consultation with the poet we have reinstated some of the key poems of the early years that have become synonymous with his name, shifted the balance of the sections and included poems from his subsequent volume of 2005 and a substantial selection of new uncollected work. Given his stature, Braun has been remarkably little translated. Some of the reasons for that are perhaps clear. The explosion of grammatical and semantic coherence, on the one hand, and the borrowing of unfamiliar forms from the German mediaeval or early modern tradition on the other; the mixture of neologisms and archaisms; the splicing of jargon, marketing slogans or Party pomp into poems, or the constant turning of German idioms, all present their challenges in English. Moreover, Braun's poetry presupposes a familiarity with East German culture and history that can seem bewildering to foreign and contemporary readers. His own collections generally include a number of brief endnotes referencing some of the historical detail. We have taken over these notes at the end of this volume and made some additions that we considered useful for an English readership. In the same vein, Braun has his particular touchstones in world literature, and many of his poems set snippets of a repertoire of especially German literature into his own context (sometimes without marking), where they work as ironic illuminations of a present plight. We have added a reference here and there where it seemed particularly helpful in shedding light on Braun's intent. Such notes are not in any way exhaustive, however. Nor, it should be said, are all those phrases highlighted in the text as apparent quotations necessarily cited from other sources. Nevertheless, at its heart, Volker Braun's is an intensely and essentially lyric project. And it is hoped that this first selection in English of over 50 years of his poetry will manage to fetch over at least some of that lyricism, rage and urgent hope to the new audience he so richly deserves.

Karen Leeder
Oxford, March 2014

1

PRUSSIA, PLEASURE GARDEN

RUBBLE FLORA

Over the rubble heaps the wild trees stand.
From the blackened stones the green leaps up like flame.
Extinguished cities. Fiery lupins and
Widows in the ruins set up house and home.

THE GRÜNDEL

1. As the path curves away into the meadow, the grass resists, we have bare feet. A body of green in the solemn sunshine. The gentle breeze is at home in the depths of the valley and dense bushes that take us in. Umbels, panicles and earth. It is enough that they sense us. Down below it is wet and the willow canes wale our backs.

2. With every year there are fewer grounds, and I feel them more deeply, to stay alive.

DEMAND

Don't come to us with it all sewn up. We need work in
    progress.
Out with the venison roast—in with the knife and the forest.
Here experiment is king, not fixed routine.
Here shout out your desires: let life provide!
Spanned between continents, towards every shore
The ocean of our hopes tenses its muscles
On every coast its fingers drum the surf
Above the waterfront its waves leap and crash
Over and over it raises up the swell and lets it fall.

It is not for us that the rules were spelt out, mister.
Life's no longer a picture book, sir, nor a tricky score,
    young miss.
From now on thinking's what's needed here.
Arses out of the arm chairs, boys: camp beds—for all I care.
Not so solemn comrades; thinking demands a cheerful mien!
Who is it longs for Wilhelmenian shoulder brass?
Our shoulders bear a heaven full of stars.

This is where new land is dug and new skies are opened—
This is a state for beginners, work in progress and that for life.
This is where you shout out your desires: towards every shore
Drum the flood of your all your hopes!
What comes crashing against your legs there, friend, the
    raging surf:
That's our little fingers, they are shooting out
Just a taste of future, child's play.

AN ACCOUNT OF DESPAIR

When she entered
And set down her empty bags on my tabletops
I felt caught out in my
Missed deeds.

The evening news dripped bloodily from the screen
And the bed stood encircled
Aside in the uninhabited zone.

She approached and embraced me
At once as though she could not be wrong

And fastened shut the door
With a black twine that had no end
And took the pictures from the wall, but there was worse:
She took the pictures out of the windows

And stopped dead in their tracks
My other friends
With her voice on the breeze
Of birds torn all to pieces.

I saw there was no arguing with this woman
She is right
Like a ruling
ONCE AND FOR ALL.

I saw all the things she held in her hands
And rose quietly like a planet that does not belong
And vanishes from the screen.

(*Fragment*)

THE LIFE AND TIMES OF VOLKER BRAUN

I was born on a Sunday and dogged by good luck:
Not blasted by bombs, nor ravaged
By the many and various hungers of the world.

In the distant drivel of the ether, in the hatred,
In the smoke from the stacks of books, the slimy stew of the
        ministries
I did not suffocate.

I grew up on the green border between town and country
That crumbles away beneath our feet.
And divide my time between thistles and compressors.

(All of this has been part of me for as long as I can remember.)

Good luck, I say. I know the taste of this rare thing.
I have opened up landscapes, worked the soil, seen the fields
        of Saxony
Grow together and desolate factories.

Yes, I can talk about good luck, the slaughter is far away.
The blows barely graze my skin.
I don't flinch, but bellow, you hear me, without shame.

Obsessed with my own small corner of home, I sense
That here the world might find an example of gentleness
Unrelenting gentleness, gentle determination.

(For that one needs the deep breathing of countless peaceful
        lungs.)

But luckily I see that this is all small beer
And my days are not filled to the very brim,
So little now the labours of my land.

How like this land I am! My fondest wishes die away.
Our gentle brains blossom too far from one another.
And the things I say. (What can I say?)

(Yet my comrades beyond the eastern borders think like me.)

I live among many others and deliver my piece.
How alone we are, I say. *What is this obsession?*
I shall not squander my life on a single province any more.

And I no longer walk easy among the many tribes
That crawl their way into a more or less Promised Land.
Divided in different ways or welding themselves together
        with steel.

(Yes, I say: in this battle to one another any sacrifice is fair.)

I, moulded from the stuff of many breeds of men
That I feel within me now, the living out of a mixed society
With mixed feelings I await my conclusions.

For a moment in the dusk I see my shinbones shining
Like dead men's bones, and I lie distant from myself
And ask myself whether I don't talk too much

Talk too much for life and limb.

AT DAWN

Every step I've still to take,
                                tears me apart.

OYSTERS

(*For Alain Lance*)

It isn't often I live really, you
For hours now in my kitchen have been opening
The immigrant (with many papers) oysters and
With a hurting hand in a plastic apron

Singing. Take the Wolfs, all they can think
Of nowadays is eating, which they do,
Like everything they do, in depth. They're human beings.
And I, with a lot of lemon, I anaesthetize

The naked little creatures then my palate
And swallow glumly. You meanwhile, with gusto and
Disgust, have slurped two dozen of these
Small cunts of the sea. Well then, I say

Let life melt in the mouth, a life
Between appetite and loathing, yes.

IS IT TOO SOON. IS IT TOO LATE

(*For Thomas Müntzer*)

Summer is at the door
The lighter time. And about us everything still
Blooming stiffly, thoughts. How ill at ease
We are when we take leave of ourselves so we
Brood instead indoors. What comrades are these,
Unlike themselves, that turn a blind eye to the
Marauding beyond the oceans
Or Prussia's puddles.

Is it too soon. Is it too late.

Tear holes in the speeches
And see how we allow ourselves
To become matchstickmen. Fling
Out those old pots, the ones we've
Always used to eat, never grown ready
To take pleasure ourselves. What is
Most joyful speak it in anger,
So we stay in our right minds.

I can do no other.

AFTERNOON

I lie naked on the sheet
With my tired face, my hands
My unruly chest
On a white sheet in the light of an afternoon
That shoots through the concrete walls
And inundates my chairs, my empty shoes.
Surprised by a sudden
Breathless vision
Of years and startled seconds, I lie naked
And overwhelmed by memories
And documents, an old man
And know neither man nor beast
In their strict differentiation
Nor the officials and censors
Of higher reason
Have I lost my mind? Or quite the opposite
I feel that I'm alive
Away from the pre-printed schedules
And fully synchronized reports
I died there, and that's the truth
As you did for me
In the obsequious dances
That freeze the flesh
But I feel I'm alive away from all that!
My fellow men, and that's the truth
On this sudden afternoon
That runs through me
And cleans me out, in my absence
On a white sheet
And fills me with its luminous
Clarity.

The search for the stuff (of writing, of living) in order, if it should come to that, to find death. To take apart the mechanisms of the age, unravel connections according to the secret blood of history. They died for the sake of public order, at work in the underground, in the poem. Prise the slogan from the teeth of death, clapped-out old bugger, where it has lost any meaning: EQUALITY. At the same time the sense of the powerlessness of words, working the streets, the world over, a lifetime long (ÉGALITÉ, GLEICHHEIT, РАВЕНСТВО) while how much? more blood must flow, blanched in the skin, rotted in the temples. What hope for me? Concepts screwed up to a pitch of tension, the speeches articles communiqués like insulating tape in my throat, so that reason does not blow a fuse. To be alone in my phrases, but knowing too that they can be searched, rifled through, pulled apart by someone else, to find the stuff that gets lost in our feelings, that leaks from our pores, an internationalist sweat. The others the same: the slow formula that must be filled with life, with what with what with what? Or with death.

ITALIAN NIGHT

Snow of poplars on the piazza / racket in the streets
Straight after the meal the pair of us fall on the
Rented bed / TORINO, GRANDE TORINO, the cries
Of delirious fans / the funeral shroud of Christ
Made ready for the fools / our soup sat under the trees
Asparagus, tomatoes and fish with our comrades / like crazy
She drapes her clothes about the room, the sheet on the floor /
Black the mark from the breast wounds and false /
And this din, I GRANTA SONO CAMPIONI D'ITALIA /
And only come to our senses with the wine naked, in the lamp-light /
Vino Dolcetto / snow of poplars on the pizza / the roofs
I see suddenly are peopled / and these looks full of desire
On the imprint of the body, the kisses / and our hands
And our feet blacken the sheet, inscribe it for real /
Snow of poplars on your lap / LA GIOIA GRANATA È ESPLOSA /
Leave the window open! says she: so we can be seen.

PRUSSIA, PLEASURE GARDEN

The grass paved over.
See how officialdom sweats, to take
The wisdom of the people, before
It can be cited, and ram
It into their hearts and minds.

FIEF

I'll hold out here, find succour in the East,
Spouting stuff that one fine day could cost
Me my neck. I'm still standing at my post.
In dwellings doled out by the magistrate
I feed my face, like all of you, on silage.
But find no joy for all my privilege.
The lodging that I seek is not a state.
With Ten Commandments and steel wire:
Oh to be with brothers, not empty spectres.

How will I survive the frozen structures.
The Party, my liege: *it gave us all we have*
Though that all does not mean our lives.
The fief I need is not awarded as a prize.

INNERMOST AFRICA

Come to a warmer land
                                with the weather of roses
And green leafy doorways
Where you will have men without disguises
For comrades.
                    Oh that is where,
With you, beloved, I should like
                               Come

out of your burrow out of your lifelong planning year
eternal
snow / waiting room where History stares at the yel-
lowing
timetable the travellers rancid / MOD land SADNESS
IS NOT ALLOWED

Under the soft tamarisks
Into the tropical rains that wash
The slogans off, the dry memoranda.

Look at the sea that is against
With cheerful waves, and into the open goes
                                oh there

No path goes that way.

When you leave, time lifts her wings.

Take the path first left through the heart
And cross the border.

Where the lemon trees are in bloom, bang, bang!

En quelque soir, par exemple, le touriste naïf EUROPE
DEAD END STATION the blacked-out trains from the
fourth world bursting with hunger / a din behind the wall
of time incomprehensible screams / blood seeps through
the sutures of defeat / the future sleets and it almost /
seems to me as in the Age of Lead

They may kill you but it may be
You will escape
Unattached and indefinite

                 come, friend, into the open!

It does not lie in the south, not abroad
Where men without disguises
Where the rains
For it is not anything vast, but it does belong to life
What it is we want
             where no one
The innermost land, the foreign land
Awaits you. You must cross the border
With your valid face.

Your red Spain, your Lebanon

Reach it before retirement.

We find ourselves, he said, on an inclined plane.
Everything points to the fact that we are going down. Just
shut your eyes and hear the way it scrapes. It is the end.
Wait and see, it will be in our lifetime. We are well on the

way. All we need do is carry on with the exercises. Not long ago, for example, we could bounce that little tally thing back above zero and say: We're on the way up! Now, no question, we're tipping into the cellar. Down among the cockroaches, ladies and gentlemen. Keep calm, go to the office, stay under cover, be brief. The terrible news has reached us, we have nothing to add. Adieu. Said the man in Itzehoe and slid from the window.

Non! We shan't spend another summer in this miserly land where we are never anything but orphans to one another promised to someone else,

come

Pearl-mussels, cicadas
Arise
Body under life sentence:
LOOK AT THE SEA, IT IS AGAINST.
REACH IT BEFORE RETIREMENT.
YOU MUST CROSS THE BORDER.

DAYDREAM

My car stood in no-man's-land between
The borderlines, handbrake on, eyed
Sternly from the watchtowers: there'd be
No changing a wheel impatiently here.

But what was I doing there? I couldn't ever
Remember being so alone; only the dead
And the as-yet-unborn breathed quietly
With me under the heat of the dog star.

The peoples were silent, but no longer slumbered
Strange days that blossomed Octoberly
Shimmering in the empty fields, waiting
Above the silence of landmines, inert.

The grim-faced future, a mulatta, doled out
Bread and work with her frugal hands
To the North and to the South, and the truth
That resides on both sides of the line.

All my life I'd known: it would come.
Now belief was all I had. And I sat still
In the grass in the cool of the evening.
Then the howling dog-handlers neared.

The laurel of mere desiring has never thrived
And our human path is errant and obscure
I must choose which side I'm on. But right now
I don't know what it is I'd say.

WALTER BENJAMIN IN THE PYRENEES

Striding calmly into the wall of fog.
Arms swing awkwardly but keeping time.
Following the scrap of paper across the precipice.
In his briefcase: dynamite, i.e.
The present

Step by step, as chance
Offers a narrow foothold
In the material. My dear lady, not to go now
That would be the real risk.
Eye on the clock / resting after five lines.

Fields where only madness runs riot.
Pressing forward with the axe in his head
I have nothing to say. Only to show.
In the smallest, clearly defined, segment.
Looking neither left nor right into
The horror

This is the method to get me there.
The vineyard crumbles, falls away vertically,
Full of dark, sweet grapes, almost ripe.
The most precious thing is the case! Body between the vines
Breathing heavily, heart

Struggling. The critical moment:
The danger that the status quo might endure.
Skeletons below, vultures above me.
Shorter steps, longer rests.

My patience makes me invincible.
Hoisting the sails of thought. Dearest lady,
Might I help myself? At the summit
Suddenly, as expected, the sheer force

Of the view. Deep blue seas:
Two at a single glance. Cinnabar coasts.
Below the cliff face, freedom

. . .

Entry denied in Portbou. But we stateless
Wanderers, we carry the fatal dose—
Would you mind holding the case—with us.

He presumably thought that he would never manage the
ascent a second time. The next morning the border offi-
cials discovered the body in my text. Construction pre-
supposes destruction. The heavy leather briefcase, saved
from the hands of the Gestapo, UNOS PAPELES MAS
DE CONTENIDO DESCONOCIDO, was lost. Too
hasty that final stroke, sir, in your life. The life bears the
work, if I may say, up this steep slope.

In every work there is a place where we feel a gust of cold
blowing towards us like the approach of dawn

DARK PLACES

In a forest without shade that stands in black
Along the bleak ridge of the Erzgebirge
I come and go in the half-light
Or is it smoke FROM BOHEMIAN WOODS AND FIELDS
Which they can't hold back at the border, grey
The grass that covers the giant's head
Where it has been rumbling on for hundreds of years
In empty galleries, where they live *as if*
In hell, and the savages toil there
With their powerful arms
                    Near Altenberg
Rising sheer above the Great Pinge, entrails
Since the earth collapsed underground
Overnight where the mine work echoed
Friend to mankind, now as then.

If that's the Mount, what about the Sermon.
The voice speaks: Turn back.—Go on! Go on—
In the dark where danger grows
From the scrub the third voice calls: MAKE WAY
The little children sledging on the Devil's Path

I always thought that this was the beginning.
Now I've spent my days in vain
And the acid rain runs down my face
Hardly breathing now, only speak this
In my dark head / my Chernobyl
Where the child in the man grows old
And the earth does not promise to endure

Freedom now and without support I stand
The voices bellowing. In the high forest
Herr Koch hangs, not a pretty sight.
DAY'S WORK IS DONE.
'TIS TIME FOR HOME. GENTLY COMES THE NIGHT

Did you use the night?—I practised hopeful
Waiting.—Who for? What for?—You also know, do you,
The pain, sweet pain, of loving the one unknown?—
The unknown deed?—You mean?—What are you
    speaking of?—
The veins were almost bursting in my flesh.
How tired I am of crossing St Mark's Square.—
Still dreaming, are you? Dreaming nevertheless?—
And the streets are waving in the winds of openness.

BREAKFAST

The loved one gave herself so easily
As though, when I had paid my life for her
By hesitating she'd hold up the transfer.
Truly I made liquid the all of me.

And what we smeared around our mouths next day
Honey and milk in the rigid restaurant—
The waiters glancing worriedly our way—
This was the stuff my lust had fastened on.

Who seeks will find, or won't. We did. And all
I had to do now like a sick man
Was take it regularly and I'd be well.
Then the proud supplier turned it off again.

The stuff of life, I've licked it, love
And salt and death are what it tastes of.

Listen friend, you would do well to take my gear. Then
you'd be a free man. And stop this harmful business. Out
of work like an oak in winter. Better an arm and a leg than
lose your neck. I will order my breakfast from the garbage
tip. Sorrel. We climb out of our beds/ Will we lose our
heads. I am the SUPERFLUOUS MAN. My living room a
car dump. HERE I STAND AND MEDITATE: SHALL I
PISS OR MASTURBATE. And that's when the light went
on and we were sitting in the dark. And I open the beer cans
in front of the TV screen, counted out / by computers the
fair game / of advertising in the thunder / of the consumer
frenzy. Tra la la. Or do you want to work the streets like my
daughters, to whom I gave away my Kingdom. The blessing
of being born too late is a rotten dowry. There are tribes
where it is a curse to be the leader. Better schizophrenic
than in two minds. For there was never yet fair time but it
made mouths in a puddle. *This is a brave night to cool a com-
munist.* Before I leave the state theatre:
When work is scarce
When the rivers flow freely in the fields
When it is spring in this state
When we reconcile ourselves with the forest
When we cease being patient as iron
When we depart in shame
When we cease murdering and being patient as iron
When we spit out our fear, the snot of betrayal
When the revolt has begun
then the women will emerge on the yellow horizon, with
their dark faces. They will be deranged, gone in the head,

and bury our compass and spit on the clocks. TOMORROW IS ALWAYS TODAY. That will be when going is used with feet. This prophecy I'll speak, for I live in my time now.

A pine tree pokes up through the runway that stretches lonely into the fields, upright relic of a forested age, how could it have taken root in the concrete, that now holds it fast in this place, the treetop splinters in the sallow light, stubborn tuft, that will not recognize the facts, from the dark edges of the landing strip a reddish trickle seeps under the lid of the sluice, blood of course, from the great beasts that are slaughtered in the fields, their brute bellowing indistinguishable from the noise of planes, or is it the howling from a theatre of war, a little off the beaten track, in the East, the loudspeakers prevent you hearing properly, and music blares into this scene too, THIS WEEK'S HITS, the MAN WHO LIVES NEXT TO THE NEW AIRPORT RUNWAY AND PREPARES THE CONCRETE FOR IT, stands leaning on his shovel and stares at his dwelling, from where the din seems to be coming, is he taking ten, has he dozed off, or is he simply out of work and stands, his own memorial, memory of great times, in his old place of work, HE HAS CAL LUSES ON HIS CHIN from the handle of the shovel, but is inured to any more digs, round about him the debris of heroic labour, waste dumps, heaps of rubbish, the WORKED-THROUGH LANDSCAPE, it is DONE FOR NOW, he stares with his wild eyes, at the bed that he has crawled out of to do his duty, what keeps him going, is there a woman behind it, for whom he redecorates the world, the person who steps out of the door now, so that the action could begin, if it hasn't already finished, she must be a BEAUTY, if you can trust the expression on his face, and he now sinks his gaze, BEAUTIFUL her arms and breasts, her thoughts, that eagerly and tenderly embrace his own, that throw themselves onto his and bring him down with her onto the cold hard floor, OVERCOME BY BEAUTY, that he sees all about him now, wherever his eyes take hold, his comfortable skin, the habit of a lifetime that he does not lay aside: where he sees beauty to throw himself at it, A MORE BEAUTI-FUL WORLD, while she keeps her eyes on him with a sympathetic smile, chin raised like a knife, skirt hiked up provocatively, her hand touches her cunt, how quickly the body picks up the thread, recalls desire as if asleep, but she's awake, watches, breaks over the sorry rest of this man, who was sent to her by the Housing Department, ALL MY HEART IS YOURS, my love, why was he unfaithful, why did he betray the starting block for the everyday race track, PHARMA BRINGS BREAD WEALTH BEAUTY, her jealousy dogs him like his own shadow, that he keeps tucked under his feet in the heart of the day, but in the evening she kneels before him dark-ened, a Negress, making him mad, LISTEN, SEE IF YOUR HEART IS STILL BEATING, and he strides over her towards this insane work of his, stamps her into the ground with his pneumatic pile-driver, man's work, hard work in the great outdoors, that begins to bloom in panic, CIVILISATURATION! MURDERERS, madness to which he is condemned and the music, cymbals and pipes, the terrible noise comes from the dancing that the women, raving like him, take from one land to the next, CORDULA I LOVE YOU! NATALIE, and from the death-rattle of the abattoirs, that seal the scene hermeti-cally, and the man, in his punishment, stirring from his antique posture, drives the edge of the shovel into his useless genitals, his balls slide onto the cement bag with a slick of blood, he lobs a grin into his white face and seems to be keeling over for ever, memorizing the course of his life back to the shimmering beginning, birth and death, in a single second the pain of freedom, turnabout to the primeval slime, freezing in white recognition, and he falls like a stone into the shadow of the pine that has rotted in the floodlight, the shadow that is mixed with the shadow of the woman, the man now a shadow too, and his seed mixes with the atoms of dust, marriage of despair, matter that learns to love in winter, flour of resurrection, dynamite in the structures, material for the hunger of the world, that comes to the door, a child's body.

From *The Zig-Zag Bridge*

THE ZIG-ZAG BRIDGE

The evil spirits can only go straight ahead
Nor can
The demon of the ideologues
Follow me into the flowering garden.

TURNING POINT

The astonishing land breeze
In the corridors. Smashed
Desks. The blood the newspapers
AND FAME? AND HUNGER
Spew up. History
Turns on its heels and is
For one moment
Determined.

THE CINNAMON FOREST

It isn't that we hold on to one another.
Only we stand together in the light
And mix it with the power of our great crowns.
And breathe softly. Even the small leaves feel

Scarcely fixed at all by the boughs they flutter round.
Not forced, not stressed, the greening factory
That runs on nothing but the gentle winds
Out of our bark produces the wild scent.

THE MUDDY LEVELS

The matchstick-men of planning
Randomly inscribed
Year after year
On the tough black damned and stinking immeasurably long
Long-suffering.

BUILDER ON THE STALINALLEE

Among the massive blocks
I come across a builder. He belongs
To the sunken classes
Who made walls that were true
And insurrections. Dreaming
I lead him back to the sweat-drenched
Scaffolding
Of a beginning.

NEW WALLPAPER

The management informs me
The alterations were completed very quietly long ago.
But the premises are no more spacious
The stairs inconvenient
And are the little rooms any lighter?
And why are people moving out not in?

People always said: If only we could do that! If only they would allow it! That'll be the day!—And now the occupiers have gone.

Not completely, it's true, there are a few left lurking in the woods; it's just that they are less conspicuous than before, they stay on in their tumbledown positions, without really taking any notice of us; they don't govern our lives any more. Their guns have presumably been useless for years now and are just waiting to be sold for scrap. This is the chosen strategy now for this incomprehensible power—that it simply surrenders: the bandages are loosened and we can move.

Ah, now we are free of chains.

But there's something: wrists heavy as lead, stooping gait, feet clumsy as if soldered on. Someone pulls the noose tight again, someone roars commands, something gasps in pain. These are the sounds of our glorious youth. There must be something in us that needs to hold on to our customary state of being (pain), our remembered feelings (hatred). We haven't been punished enough. That dark suspicion all along, that it might be functioning by itself, at least in what we recall of the last fifty years, seems to have been proved right. We are it. Calculated to the nth degree, methodical, the torture machine. We must be destroyed, pulverized, swept from the face of the earth. There must be an end to it. What have they done to us? But now the next question: What are we going to do?

I

How obscure is the material
Of the world. Together with the storms and floods
The inevitable earthquakes
Come quakes of the peoples and
The landslide of thought.

For years it seemed as though the times
Stood still. The clocks were full
Of sand of blood and the stagnant day
That dawns once more
As Judgement Day and out of the blue.

Where are we headed or, put more modestly,
Does anyone know their elbow from their arse?
Strategies go rotten
Like tents dismantled in a deluge
Behind the refugees.

States, their future built up! Sunk
Into the grass they feed on. Rock-solid
Alliances waver as they wade in bogs and blood
Indissoluble friendship
Eyes up its waste water
Suspiciously.

There they've ignored the hunger for communism
    and demand

Proper middle-class cuisine; and there
They wipe the slate of history clean and stand
              before an empty plate.

But consider
That the hunger that holds sway there
With the mandate of the masses is the hunger
For justice.

II

Our state now trumpets its successes as if it had been won
from the ocean. In truth it was an ocean of ruins. But the
rubble women are bent double like a monument and round
the pedestal the bulldozed landscape fills with sand. From
a distance perhaps it resembles a massive dune: happy hol-
idays in the revolution. The inhabitants hold out and wait,
with their always identical gestures and tense faces as if they
were expecting a miracle, while the goal grows pale in the
darkness of its own shadow, faced with the floodlight of
western temptations. They see themselves carried to an
island that is battered by currents that sweep everything
away or is it the high tide of a turbulent spring? And they
dig breakwaters in their meadows or rush blindly for seats
on the last Icarus to leave.

III

SPRINGLOADED GUNS. THE SHOCKING CLARITY
    OF WORDS
FIRE IN THE LETTERBOX

UNDER THE WALLPAPER THE FISSURES
IN THE SUBSTANCE
TOUCH ME!
THE VEINS BREATHE IN THE ROCK.

IV

Our stage, offering space
For the great contradictions
Is open once more.
The wagon of the woman peddling wares
And the comrades' iron truck
Collide. What ancient vehicles
That permit no turning! Their patent
Difficulties encourage us
To try another kind of movement. Let's
Open dialogue
About the turn in this land of ours.

2

THE MASSACRE OF ILLUSIONS

O CHICAGO! O CONTRADICTION!

Brecht, did you let your cigar go out?
During the earthquakes that we induced
In those states that were built on sand.
Socialism's out the door, but here comes Johnnie Walker.
I can't grab it by the principles
That are shedding anyhow. The warm streets
Of October are the chilly byways
Of market economics, Horatio. I wedge my gum in my check
And there it is, your nothing-much-worth-mentioning.

PROPERTY

That's me still here. My country's going West.
WAR ON THE POOR GOD BLESS THE PALACES.
I helped it out the door with all the rest.
What paltry charms it has it gives away.
After winter comes the summer of excess.
And I *can go to hell* is what they say.
I don't know the meaning of my text.
What I never owned, they've taken even this.
What I never lived, I know I'll always miss.
It was hope that came before this fall.
My property, you flog from stall to stall.
When will I say *mine* again and mean of all.

9 NOVEMBER

Lengths of wire, the brackish water has a barbed smile
Silently, like a dream, the mines drift
Like dinner plates back into the cupboard. Surreal moment:
On tiptoe where the world is sundering, and not a shot.
Reason, so long hounded, utterly fagged out, reaches
For some (any old) mistake . . . The filthy bandage bursts.
Neon signs invade to centre stage. REJOICE
BERLIN, too soon. Blow now, nor'easter, hard.

MY BROTHER

The beggar on the greasy steps of the BANCO DI ROMA
On a piece of corrugated cardboard BROTHER, curled
In his cap at noon. How am I better off than him?
Nothing but my verses feeds me and gets me a bed.
My lines, my sores, cover the paper, filthy
And exposed. Shameless words
That live on the streets, begging for sympathy.
A skinny boy with his hand out
Staggers from human being to human being
For some humanity. The gypsies in the exhaust fumes.
Not even by a hope am I better off than you.

The dead behave as they always do,
Stepping out at night into the graveyard at Rotoli
The same old weapons and words. It's all they know.
The blood drains into the Mediterranean. They erect ruins.
CARTHAGE NEW YORK. The mighty
Left elbow of Jupiter in the museum at Tunis
He needed them both to secure his victory.
But if only the living could . . . never mind.
YUPPY SCUM. JUST STUFF THEIR MOUTHS
    WITH SOMETHING TASTY
And its game over. In any case, I'm of the opinion
That socialism must be destroyed, and
I like my causes lost.

AMBRA

Why are these men lying on their backs?
Or playing dominoes mornings in the medina?
That there dressed in black flits past
And kneels in a field with a stone on the soil.
But the man smokes a hookah through his plumped-up lips.
No doubt at night he has three women in his bed
And they are gentle with him as with something precious
Scented, that slips between the fingers
A belief that, thought about, evaporates.
But he takes them carelessly like scoured cactus figs.

Statues with nooses round their necks, posterity's
Personnel Department changing its unpersons: Gorbachev
Who scattered an empire to the winds, the corpse of Stalin
Visits him four-thirty a.m. in the Crimea,
On the sober stomach of the people and dines
Afterwards with Yeltsin: the tablecloth the tricolour
THE IRON RATION OF CONSCIOUSNESS SCOFFED.
THAT, COMRADES, IS THE FEAST OF FREEDOM
Before the display panel of tin cans;
As sure as camels stare into the sun
We will stand eye to eye with truth or meet
Our end in the desert of resistance.

MARLBORO IS RED. RED IS MARLBORO

Sleep now, rest . . . But you lie awake, smiling.
Only my body is still underway
On one road or another and alas where to?
You wanted to encompass the unknown.
I know all that now. All that is the desert.
Desert, you say. Or I say affluence.
Enjoy, breathe, eat. Offer your hands open.
I'll never live towards a turningpoint again.

I

Cheerful grey: the Atlantic sky,
                    a bank of cloud
          On which your gaze 'reclines'
               Into the context
Light streaming down extravagantly
And the forms
          in tatters
                    of the thoughts
               Continuing the struggle (for what?), the *dead ideas*
     In aerial combat
                         (half armour half body)
A Catalaunian field. The muzzle blast
          Of the morning paper
That you inhale bent over the table
          With your laughing eye, Cyclops

Having no enemies!
                    with limbs relaxed
          In the undivided water, spawn-smell
               Of birth and death, millennial silt.
The shattered bunkers steeply
               Hanging on the naked shore:
A cloud-burst, diagonal hatching,
                         removes the things begun
Beyond recovery . . .
                    an exhausted front.

II

Striding forth on the steep downhill of *progrès*
    There was no hold or halting any more
        A fissure
Through existence (. . .) The minefield
            Of your compromises
    Slowly explodes. *Passé*
Political animal
Forget the scent of the goal.
Wound up
    ruled out
        fallen away
With no central perspective
Your lightweight body drops through the grid;
PARTY AND STATE, the abrupt come-down
Of the roped-together
    From the North Face of the Eager
      Into nothing—

And only this woman with bare breasts
    ('the last hold')
        Looking the worse for pleasure, bravely
      With the hormone plaster on her hip
Is left you for a refuge:
        quit that place too!
A brash beguiling
Thrust into the heart's flesh
Fini. But you hold on
Tight,
    with two fingers
    At the wrist, reckless insistence
On your opinion . . . ancient revolt
      Tenderness.

III

Suddenly you were on West Shore, scented trees
      With cones as big as grenades
    Heat-fields: further
You cannot go in this direction, you have
      Passed through
          the great breadth of France
     (*This madness*! *This promise*!)
           'a trek from the German North-East'
On the autoroute. *Roulez relaix*. The brochures
        Of your desire, with pictures
   From real life
          DOUX ET RÉSISTANT
Like toilet paper. What a quick end
    To the long march.
      You take in the air
The one slogan:
      That is it. / 'That was it.'

The suicide on the railway line
     (Homeless. . . . 'it is not known why')
The body bled empty, like a white sculpture
      The skull opened up
      The red cavity
    Which I contemplate, *an opportunity*
     Extreme
As love which stakes all on the one card,
               in the end
He enjoyed the same noise, a rolling
    Definitively
Like the sensations
    of ebb and flow.

IV

Or dug up out of the sand, Althusser
        Lacking more powerful arguments
Struck it dead, his ONEANDALL,

                                the chattering
                doctrine, large as life.
Let go, and where to!
                then with your arms
Unhappy man. Sartre
        In the empyreum shyly gives him his hand
                (His monument stands, a bog body
                        All by itself). The beyond
Was small concern of ours
        The same (at best) in green

From our island utopia
                (common ownership!
        Money: not important, work for all)
Expelled for want of imagination,
                        incapable of enjoyment
Failed
        Real existences, *total mobil*
    In the *prétexte* of simulation. We
(It talks, it can't stop talking
        And being right, it is only a matter of years
Then he struck it dead)

                No more suggestions. Drive
        The problem out and let it stand
Like a dead thing
                in your biography.

V

Breakfast, 'Waiter, the traffic menu, please'
   . . .
They crouch on the flats like comical birds
     Claws out downwards
           Plastic bags like black
       Craws, swags, the grubbers for mussels
In La Tranche-sur-Mer. Lonely lascivious work
Of poets,
      for a crude meal.
                What does
    The End of History
            Count in this everyday silt
Where above is below and death life.
    . . . And he used the time pondering
       The paradox
         That we enjoy being hit
'Pokes in the ribs . . . gratefully accepted.'
      In a woman's face
He reads, opens what can be opened
    The mouth, the eyes, he reads
      More in a woman's face.
Boiling water. They slurp the mussels
     Night after night
     Stunned with lemon
And again I hoped of the things
    I encounter
      As a chosen one
        To show myself worthy.

VI

A midday without an address, fleeing the wind and sick
    For sun you stray
        Out of this gulf of politics
            ('given back
To life') into the flowering steppes. Would you
    (Or anyone for you) ever
Have dreamt it? Like a girl
    Your soul, wandering the mudflats, freed
        From the petrol pumps
You can sense the equal buoyancy of the land masses
    On the pulsing core of the earth. *Change of subject.*
        Cannibalism among the galaxies
            You can say you are there. The plate tectonics
Of history ('like a rear-end collision')
    And the supercontinent
        Pangaea arises
            COCA COLA out of the ocean.
Now you have everything (that you don't need), relax

The change of the seasons sixty times
    Thrice the change of an era
You won't do it for less;
                take
    Things as they're not any longer
With cold respect: not a passer-by . . .

                    en passant.

VII

Naked mattresses, mildewed, shamelessly
　　On an iron double bed
Rammed in between the door and the window
Submissive under our weight. To catch the eye
　　A festival of the nymphs from the *patronne*'s
　　　　Stock, a smell of copulations
Countless times repeated like the wallpaper's check pattern
　　A slop of passions
Kitchen knives and sweat. In this

Great setting I confess my gaiety
　　And all else I am guilty of
　　　　(The feeling
Complice, is not used up IN USE
　　Like a bar of soap . . . Wash yourself in guilt)
Snuggling against a back
　　In the moment
　　　　Of greatest seriousness
Out of which you come forth,
　　　　　　a dead man or a man in love
　　('He has paid')
Transformed into a bastard
Of accidents and races
And the ecstasies
　　of the becoming possible
　　Hidden in the heart of the magic enthralling you all
A morning that wet with dew opens the shutters.

VIII

Rolling back onwards into normality
    Bumper
        to bumper
            (*And I, whither*?), the blockade
Before Fontainebleau. The bonds-
    Men in their tumbrils resting
Until they croak. STANDSTILL, o
Detention in the column, serene
Hours of truth,
        vision of a static city
'I live: I examine the materials of life'
(Virilio)
        All around, the abandoned countryside.
In the forest of Barbizon
           the war of pictures
    The travellers with no arrival
'The tourism of desperation'
    the pastose manner, in engine oil.
That it carries on like this, he knew, is a catastrophe.
And he
    squatted amid the splendid ancient trees
        And could shit
And went back to those at rest, back into
Things as they were, altogether,
           painted by Millet.

And the fire on the edge
    Of this text continuing to devour itself

IX

Chinese sliver grass in German fields / the landowners
    Trample the morning acres flat,

                              as after

    The point of your life
The residual sweetness of a large meadow

I alone remain burning in the shadows (. . .)

BALANCE

1

Her youthful body, soft and warm her breast
The unmade bed. The whole damn lot unreal,
I should have known that it would come to this
But I am torn to shreds. And that same year

The state came tumbling down. Not a man
Left standing on his neighbour. I was empty
Being and certainly consciousness down the pan
The world to the dogs, what did it matter to me

On which shoulder I carry it? On both
Whether I stand or fall. I keep my balance

2

And then at some point later, the *realization*, sitting in
the Gaukbehörde, in Normannenstraße, three weeks
listening to JosephandhisBrothers on the car radio, the
files do the rest, rummaging in the entrails, yours mine;
that's when I lost it

PLINY SENDS GREETINGS TO TACITUS

(For Heiner Müller)

Why did Pliny make for the centre of the catastrophe
When the cloud rose up in the shape of a pine
White and filthy as the elements it had dragged aloft
As a man of science he thought the matter
Worth a closer look. He called for his sandals
Launched the quadriremes and with a favourable wind
Bore towards Vesuvius *dirt and red-hot pumice*
Why did he not remain at a safe distance
At his card-table in Misenum
He knew the *true nature* of the upheaval
Harmlessly verdant to the summit, the peasants
Settle in the ashes of their hopes
When the memory cools and is able to calculate
As you know, land prices have risen again
Pliny the Younger writes to Maecilius Nepos
Because the Princeps has obliged the candidates
To purchase land before their election
A dwelling place in the Empire country houses under the volcano
The risks of the political cinder-track, why
Did he want to know exactly *He hurried*
Where others were fleeing from, directly into the danger
Dictating to a scribe all the images of the disaster
While the sea withdrew and chunks of stone were falling
In his complete *Natural History* (37 volumes)
He had foretold the event and the end of the world
Which now was reduced to his own
A man of my age with an insatiable curiosity *He*

Had himself carried to the bath, dined quietly and lay down
In the horror, his breathing, because of
His corpulence, audible
Why did I remain in the midst of the catastrophe
Of my century *The betrayed Revolution*
With all the traitors who wished to know it betrayed
I thought the matter worthy, etc. *They fastened cushions*
On their heads for protection against the falling stones
I knew the true nature of the upheaval
Planted with red flags to the summit, the workers
And peasants scrabbling in the mud of promises
I have described (in volume after volume) the downfall
Only now and then a mouthful of cold water
And the end will only be my own
Meanwhile I bathe and eat
Of the dross of another catastrophe
The Triumph of the West by J. M. Roberts
Observed close up a natural phenomenon
Till the debris reaches the doorstep crushingly
Why do I not abide
At my desk in my certain hope
Only now and then it was necessary
To shake off the ash so as not to be buried
The steamrollers of progress *breathtaking*
They stopped his throat The ash of Auschwitz
The dark cloud in the shape of a mushroom
Leaping from the ground, why do I go on with the exercise
In the cold lava of the revolution
In the Nile mud of civilization
In a four-door wreck of an automobile
In the exhaust fumes of Naples

THE MAGMA IN THE HEART OF THE TUAREG

With a German passport landing at Agadir
In the winter sun: a change of identity
Slaves are watching me and thieves
Prowling about my feet, who am I
A nomad in the four-star hotel, room with a view of the sea
I can choose my season
LEISURE IS EPIDEMIC even in the gear
Of a tourist I'm on the dole and hanging around
In the last-minute lands LIFE-LONG
The throw-away man, only COCA COLA needs me
The tea-drinkers of Marrakesh have still to be converted
To the global gods, and I
No longer driven to find the place and the solving word
I belong to all the useless peoples.

6. 5. 1996

I overslept in the Art Hotel, it was raining
Cats and dogs into the Elbe, no breakfast
But a hungry look at the walls
Penck, offspring of no class in particular, has painted
    himself a museum
Hunting scenes for cavedwellers ART OF THE WEST or
THE MATCHSTICK-MEN OF PLANNING, the taxi
Got stuck in the traffic on the Dimitroff the Augustus Bridge
Nothing functioned while my mother died
I went on foot, rounding a piledriver
A tool that belonged to Antaeus a land speculator
From Libya with his subcontracted workers
The city was torn up like after the air-raids
Baroque rubble, you can stroll in the foundations
And look for the error, in the Chancellory
A dumb pushing and shoving, static artists
They hold out whatever the government
Adam Schreier Güttler Hoppe and Braun
GO AND SEE HIS HIGHNESS WHEN
HE ASKS YOU TO, AND ONLY THEN
King Kurt the Early Riser
Summoned the still sleepy Academy
To a morning roll-call, my tiredness
Has a more complicated origin, I yawn
From more epochs, my mockery is a late vintage
From the slopes of my consciousness
In the place of my instant dismissal
We printed FRÖSI sing and be joyful
Four colours offset TRUE, IF THE CHILDREN
WERE ALWAYS CHILDREN my wideawake brother

Confirmed my political immaturity
The second went over the border without a licence
One of five, that was only realistic
I carried a suitcase for the daughter of a musician
She wanted to study music without politics
Wide awake to the station after a night of love
In the land of Hanns Eisler, a struggler in vain
Against STUPIDITY IN MUSIC
On the way home I became a poet in Germany
Among the stubblefields under a starry sky
A muddy path under my feet, or sand at least
On the corridors of power, my gentleness
Was hard won in the cement factory SOCIALISM the
    question
Abiding no answer or, as it might be, the answer
Abiding no questions, now in Moscow
The Synod has met to discuss the question
CAN THE APOCALYPSE HAPPEN IN ONE COUNTRY?
And the joke has worn thin, gone bust as it seems
Goldmann, my feet are going to sleep
On the parquet floor, we were awake too long
Too awake with waiting for the morning
Until it dawned on us that the morning had been and gone
I was drinking champagne in the Saxon Academy
While my mother was dying, I saw her yesterday
Life in her wasted body, pain
Was twisting her into her last shape, for a moment
She had lost her courage and was tired
A chance to MAKE HER COMFORTABLE, she lay
With her head back and in puzzlement /
Rage she was lifting her arm with the tube stuck in it
And felt at her face and the oxygen mask

Not knowing we were there / not being able to move, today
We find her removed to the cellar, hard by
The door, her chin bound up, her head
Little as a mummy's, a scrap of gauze on her eye
Still lying, and her cheeks are cold
I've got another thirty years to live
I'm sitting at a table with my dead father
It's barley-soup, the soldier spoons it up
His gun on his shoulder, the soup tastes salty
From the tears that in secret over the stove
Have been mixed in, or twenty
If I don't get tired, fed artificially
By the times I live in EAST WEST
A MIXTURE says Penck BELOW ABOVE
Speedy deliveries in red and black acrylic
No a separation IN AND OUT
LIFE AND DEATH, when will the poet
Be born, AFTER YEARS OF DEFEAT
AND GREAT UNHAPPINESS WHEN THE SLAVES
    BREATHE AGAIN
AND THE IMAGES AWAKE AT THE STUPENDOUS
    VISION.

From his tumulus Caesar watched
The distant sea battle *Barbarian ships* cold sweat
Of a great man making history *After that it was a matter*
Of courage and billhook
Ripping down the yards and the leather sails
BELLUM GALLICUM the usual Gulf War
Played out before the eyes of the land army in their
      seaside cinema
And the sudden drop in the wind
That's how empires are made / I've seen them fall
Standing on his bones the Führer's bunker
Grotewohlstrasse in the other Germany
The astonishing land breeze in the corridors
History blinks so as not to be blinded
Uncertain rapture DANCING ON THE WALL
The wall-peckers with their little hammers
The *Volksarmee* observes the ranks of the unemployed
One minute in this time of Mine

Inhabited by sea squalls and salt tides, the bay is the meeting place of the deceased. It swills them here, from the courses of their failed lives, the empty rivulets, from their broken boats, with the keels jutting out of the sand. Since memory began they've been lying there in piles, *little dunes of bone-white sand*, sinking down deeper, only reluctantly making way for the new arrivals that are flung on top of them. They are never really *buried*. They wait while they still have their bones or their wits about them to be transported across to the Isles reserved for the Blessed. That's the longing that takes hold of us all when we fetch up here. The Blessed are those who are proved right in life as they are in death. I witnessed that triumph myself: as we, long after our own downfall, were raised up by history and *vindicated*. As though drunk, intoxicated, we wallowed in the unexpected swell. The beaches thronged with the cheering millions! But when we came to the surface, we met with only bitterness and recrimination. Hostile stares turned us away; we had not been summoned. What did we have to reproach ourselves for? What was our crime? Wanting to change the world that had now gone under. Now we were greeted with jeering and laughter. We were the traitors, who had given them hope. That was the fate of many of the dead: the history where they had triumphed had disappeared. Now we were scum. Mad world: now we who had fought against it were to blame that it had existed at all. We laughed, gurgling in the swill. But salvation was at hand, they were building us a bridge to the Islands. Now just go they said (everyone knows this voice), take all your hopes and leave us alone. Admit it: you're dead and betrayed. That much was true. We took a deep breath. It's red and it is bloody, renounce it. Bury the flag. *Nothing will ever change.* And then you will be among the Blessed, who exit the stage to applause. We heard the words that came so easily and gazed across at the Islands. There we would find peace. We could bury our cause for ever. We heard ourselves laughing and the gurgle resounded across the bay. The dead looked up with their dead eyes and held their breath, as they had, of course, for so long. Yes, we said, it was wrong. And we'll be across. But not wrong from the outset and not always.—What, you miserable wretches, don't you want to be saved.—Not under those conditions, not at any price. That's what we said, and even as we were still laughing we felt ourselves sinking deeper, down to the bottom, to the lost, to those who had not given in, and I hereby commit this to the record.

AFTER THE MASSACRE OF ILLUSIONS

Guevara under the runway with his hands
Hacked off, he doesn't 'work i' the earth' any more so now
The ideas are buried
Out come the bones
State funeral FOR FEAR OF RESURRECTION
O Sacred Head Sore Wounded Marketing
FOLLOW YOUR FINE PHRASES
TO THE POINT OF THEIR INCARNATION
Valery Khodemchuk, covered up
In the sarcophagus of the reactor, can wait
How long will the earth endure us
And what shall we call freedom

LAGERFELD

Rome: an open city A laager
Down the catwalk troop the fashions
Of the millennium, bulletproof vests
For copulation Two gladiators
Are fighting for the job, long practised
In the tricks of throttling, they win applause
That's what they went to school for HIM OR ME
The stink of fear In his empire
Lagerfeld is making a dream come true A PACK
OF WOMEN THE PICK OF BEAUTY
The winter collection for the wars in Dacia
Has made him rich IT IS ENOUGH TO TURN YOUR
    STOMACH
They are bearing my ideas, these are summer clothes
To the spoilt world A festival of beauty
Helena Christensen in evening wear Meanwhile
The two craftsmen have not let go
One is Commodus, the wild son
Of a cool father, the mother's indiscretion
When he croaks the throne stands empty
And Septimius Severus the African
Will march with the XIVth from the wilderness of Vienna
Against the capital POOR ROME A barbarian
Emperor On his heels the rest of the world
Lagerfeld doesn't watch He has a problem
He can make them more beautiful but not better
More and more beautiful Outfit of the brute beasts
RICH AND POOR A divided clientele
ATROCIOUS Paying and thieving
I enjoy undivided attention But

He knows what's going on, he isn't blind
The fifteen-year-old killer from Springfield
A MOUNTAIN OF CORPSES IN THE HIGH-
	SCHOOL CAFETERIA
He has learnt to lend a hand
He is in custody now in paper clothes
Another fashion From America gangs of children
Are combing North Rhein-Westphalia trainees
Looking for food at Hertie's and Woolworth's
A light-fingered tribe from the future
In the employment exchanges carrion
Is waiting to be recycled It will wait a long time
Those in work are waiting on machines
The others are waiting to be allowed to wait on something
Legions While the world turns black
As Africa VIOLENCE MUST NOT ONLY BE
	THREATENED
IT MUST ALSO BE USED The Foreign Office
Inwardly grinning states its position
On Bosnia We'll show you what work is
A machine with limbs sexually neutral
The mannequin for tomorrow's work
AT THE END OF THE DAY YOU ARE A JUST
	ANOTHER PRODUCT
Thinking is, precisely, what I try to avoid
Day after day the covering of paper with print
Custody, to prevent the suicide of the species
I don't read it, I don't watch
A theatre full of equanimity
THE ONLY PLACE I FEEL AT EASE
DESPAIR Kleist on the edge
At Stimming's Inn MY ONE TRIUMPHANT CONCERN

TO FIND A DEEP ENOUGH ABYSS he lends a hand
Two dots near Potsdam Waiting for nothing
That's the drama: there is no action
We know otherwise and refrain from action No
We can do no other The dress
Fits like a second skin NOWADAYS THEY DO
    EVERYTHING
IN HUMAN FLESH Goes on and on
Look at Commodus, a death off the peg /
Lagerfeld or Serenity He
Doesn't love the beauties he can have His heart
Seeks beauty everywhere Beauty
Is a son of the gutter, has previous convictions
See here, his description, black skin
I enjoy the luxury of having been expelled
An idiot in the third millennium A citizen of the world
Helena Christensen leaves the catwalk
Why should I become fashionable
In the throwaway society
The arena full of the last screams Ideas
Rome's last era, unseriousness
Now watch the finale ME OR ME
Greetings, barbarians

COINED FOR THE RULING CLASS

You workers and farmers, pampered heroes
Of labour and waiting, outstanding inventors
Of the Land of Cackaigne, guilty of shitty humility
The victory speech will say of you: they feared nothing
Not even their own expropriation. The medal
Will be pinned to your chests.

Classical coinage, polished by Cavafy, newly minted in
the 10th year after Ourgreatfkin'leaders

From *Dances of Death*

She has nothing better to do than nothing at all
It's a job just staying alive, from hand to mouth
A spectre from the future living on the dole
Singing in Soho! Bed of roses! The daydream
Of walking upright on the umbilical cord
Of a can of beer. PROGRESS IS AT HOME
IN CATASTROPHE. So that's what the shat-on
Have to hope for. Dancing in the morning
With the populace, shopping malls set alight
Thrown out, she's nothing else to do but better.

COMMUNISM

An artist, working in refuse, the hunger
Of the world, weak at the knee, empty
Of ideas, no more slogans in his gob:
The very sight of him incites, sets them
Alight in the stinking slums TO EACH
ACCORDING TO HIS NEED (the classic texts,
Forbidden ones, sent out into the streets)
The REAL MOVEMENT down down
The easy thing so very hard to achieve
Another spectre that is haunting our world

COMMON OWNERSHIP

You still recall what once belonged to all
And none? COMMON PROPERTY. Landslide
After the plebiscite, and into the abyss
A new epoch and a brand-new car.
MADNESS. Meet up in the bargain basement
All spick and span and I'm your man and up
For almost anything, King Customer. It's pick 'n' mix
Poundland style. EVERYTHING AND NOTHING
Was it ever really yours? Fuck you, fantasist.
The encore: all that you could never need!

And who's that waltzing in, bang on cue
STILLBORN. Two bits short of a bite, ghost
Of a world view. What does she eat away in you
The crust of opportunism. A one-track mind
On day-release in a one-horse happy hour.
Skips on tiptoes through the lakes of blood
Or water, what difference would it make.
Her dealer dishes the daily dose of red-top dirt
She babbles NATO NATO not a word of sense
Just over and over till she hits the deck.

CLASS STRUGGLE

Rumoured dead, he turns up in disguise
Among the mourners at the wake. Bought off
With pennies, profit rates ('going down')
Last rites administered by Vodafone.
Well-liked, for sure, but kidding no one
With this fatal fit-up in the lab.
Child trafficker, unionized organ donor
THE HISTORY OF ALL HITHERTO, etc. Corruption.
Just take a look at the obits. Death and apotheosis.
If only the bastard would croak, once and for all!

SOLIDARITY

She's even forgotten her name, loss of memory
After the blood. Out for a lark, on the march
The pale beauty, no idea to whom she now belongs:
To men? Mankind? Or to the dogs. Most like
The dogs that are snapping at her heels.
Backward and forgetting, with no food or with plenty.
This weakness! Good that her partner takes the lead
It's Death, as usual. Though this might be her own.
Now she's lobbing bombs for human rights
ALL OF US OR NONE. On the march. Fuck that for a lark.

ART

She dances on the graves, with grace
With her rogue memory. WE KNOW
WE CAN'T HOLD ON TO ANYTHING. She
Calls up the croaked, the forgotten, them
With their knives and demands. Love
Gone out, anger gone cold, the wasted times. What
Is the thought that we are mortal set against
THE GREAT IN VAIN? She dares to think it
Underground where everything lives. How
Is it possible that things the way they are
Are dancing?

3

FINDINGS

PONTINE MARSHES

At a bay in the mudflats I saw the pair
Together kneeling by a mound of mud
They worked it gently with their bare hands,
Just as gently dribbling mud with their
Fingertips that found one another there
Lascivious and slippery with clay so that
Together they were building something
Bit by bit. A tower of tenderness taking
Shape that passers-by kept stopping to admire:
Was it gravity or love that moved them more?
And yet it grew so close to the water
That every wave would wash it clean
Away.—What are you setting out on?
There'll be nothing left of your art or your love.—
They weren't the slightest bit deterred.

PARADISO

The night fell fast. A glow worm lit our path
Back and forth in a rickety Fiat without springs
That spilt out six people at the very least
Into the mountains that grew downwards
And were flooded from above by warm torrents
That took us by surprise and sent us over.
Naked as we were on the naked belly of the cliff!
It roared and sprayed from the stony dugs.
I sat, and not alone, in a shallow trough
In which the cross-current did its work
So that I slid, in all innocence, without
Embarrassment, just the force of water
Into her, who? And from above the pressure
Of the spate pushed me in—out. Angels' work.
And falling deeper, dawn crept up the sky.

BERLIN-MITTE

It was a graveyard where we ended up
And her wild lips buried into mine.
And all around us everything was still
Though we couldn't get enough of
Calling out our names: my love! my lover!
And on the graves: Love lasts for ever!
Till desire felled us amongst the stones.
Mickel who'd knocked back his red wine
Was toking on his laurel down below.
This is where I want to lie, in peace
A graveyard is where we'd all end up
I was sure, so I buried my lips
In hers. And, as if drunk on life,
She wrapped her legs around me hard, and I
Saw black earth below and above me only sky.

TIDES

I

Floods I saw this year
Forest fires
Sea and state-quakes,
A shrug of the shoulders force nine

2

Hybrid things of bone and wire
Hands like an iron dog cramp
In the red light line-up
Such is the company I keep.

3

The cement mixer rolls the dice: grass or stone
Hungry Hennecke
Hasta la vista / gizza job mista
Shot himself in the foot
Lives hand to mouth. Good luck!

4

And fresh sustenance, new blood
Learn the art of harmless reading,
Son; the little leaves begin to drift
After days like these
A vale of joys,
This life of ours.

I can see clearly once again and my two eyes
Concoct a perfect world. I don't mind their lies
And like to contemplate the grave and all its fears.
If that's my lot, I'll praise the world as it appears.

> *How can you say to me, I am a king?*
> *Our scene is alter'd from a serious thing*
> (Richard II)

On the flight across the Atlantic the paper from home
A man Happily Unemployed writes to the unhappily
    employed
I to myself ABOUT THE TACTICS OF DOING NOTHING
I'm sitting in the Boeing seat belt fastened
Drinking whisky among the scraps of cloud
Weather fronts markets tumbling turbulence
WE WILL OURSELF IN PERSON TO THIS WAR
The declaration of war is a commercial break
I shop therefore I am Not a blade of grass
Nor a single leaf finds its way up here but plastic cups
I am happily occupied overtaking time
And all my beliefs from a rusty age
WHAT IS TO BE DONE must concede I am defeated.
The premium trash in the Economy Class a battlefield
Le bateau ivre on a scheduled flight
Awash with metaphors On England's coasts
The cattle are burning Madness is holding court
The stewardess serves the meal. What do you have.—
    Casserole.—
Is it beef?—Human meat.—Hunger forces it down.
A ragged band from Kosinzew's LEAR extras
From MOSFILM straggling across continents
What's wrong with them. Migraines.—They are migrants.
Germany for the Germans and Put the fun back into flying
HOW SHALL WE DO FOR MONEY FOR THIS WAR

Of course the forest is receding and we are not born of
     woman
The state is BANKRUPT and the country leased out
And I public enemy must come to terms
With it and wish everyone GOOD MIGHT

'The world is getting smaller', Aafke Steenhuis says and looks
out of the twelfth floor of the Plaza. 'We're living too fast.'—'In
freefall through evolution.'—What is there to hold on to? Love,
a man?' She moved with her child from a house of stone to a
houseboat, 'And power?'—A floating clinic off the coast of
Dublin. Abortion in international waters!' She still has milk and
yesterday saw a baby crying in its pram and considered feeding
it herself, the father hissed: Don't touch! 'I would have done it
in Brazil, where they dance the samba after work until the traffic
jams die down.' She forgot to eat and couldn't find a cafe late at
night so fed herself with her own milk and I asked her if she
knew Erica Jong's fucked-up idea for curing starvation in India

Or in the BIG BROTHER house A black guy
Rapes the nice middle-class girl
Under cover of publicity The channel announces their
     engagement
My friend the fool living in two worlds
With one head, now he can forget one of them
And how are you, István.—I'm good.—And really.—Bad.
He's putting on JOB a backstage comedy The dust
Of Egypt is the smoke of Auschwitz
The Biblical cloak the uniform of the camp
Off the rack. Now they won't believe that God
Has had them tailor-made, what luxury A passenger
INCAGED wedged into such a narrow space

THE WASTE IS NO WHIT LESSER THAN THY LAND
Discovers something. The cockpit is empty
Strange, we already know. It doesn't surprise us
Hobsbawn is leaning by the door and cracks a joke
We don't know where we're headed.—From a short
Century into a meaningless one
A journey without a fixed goal
Bateau ivre abandoned by its tugboats
The metaphor swigs at life POETRY DISHWATER
Rimbaud an abdicated King
NOW MARK ME HOW I WILL UNDO MYSELF
My Lord, no more, but that you read these grievous crimes
Mine eyes are full of salt tears, yet you traitors here
I see and find myself a traitor with the rest
Who hastily sets down his handwritten note illegible
MYLORD DISPATCH READ O'ER THESE ARTICLES

And Ann Marlowe, sitting on a chair in Manhattan gazing into the distance, where I am going under, and opens her legs. 'Again, once more', I whisper, 'a society that is opening up!'— 'You wordy tosser, come on.' She braces her knee against the punter's flies. Investment banking and drugs, I've lost the plot, but it's no big deal, I guess. Catastrophes will pave the way. 'Get on with it, or finish yourself off,' she laughs. 'That thought is stronger that incorporates another thought.' And she waves for the waiter and when he arrives at the table, she shoves the lighter in her mouth. The suicide staggers out and with both hands she lifts up her tits for me

What kind of shuttle scuttle of shitty rubble do we have here
The landing strip a landfill site FORTALEZA Swarms
Of kids graze the rubbish heap in a race with vultures
An old woman strides though puddles of piss head held high

The dosser in front of the SCHLAFLAND store
    PowellStreet San Francisco
High-rise beds for vacationing nations
To do or not to do, that is no question
SHOPPING AND FUCKING Please arrange
A proper execution for the relatives of the victim
The century bled dry
By images camps and beaches
Death a tourist The King a customer
I don't have to think for long before comparing the earth / jail
And because the slammer's full I am in the community
Woman man my brain begetting thoughts
Progress is not better but it's different
I'm in the mood and won't be done
Until everything is gone
Towards noon it gets noticeably cooler, then darkness
Falls from above as announced
I see the end of the world as per usual The blockbuster
The solar eclipse over Reims Or the superbomb
I WASTED TIME AND NOW DOTH TIME WASTE ME
A man without power involuntary outcast
In a worn-out world sees bewildered
That he's still alive, breathing air, walking the earth
On tender soles after me
In the light rain my light grave

Postscript after 11 September 2001

The attack on the towers of the World Trade Centre
The renown of a mega-city in the dust
Lower Manhattan runs into the tip of the iceberg
Atta atta the children shout
Terror in the text The text in terror

WORLD POWER

Your monument is great, Augustus—I write on
      fleeting scraps—
What's that? I write, a lizard scurries across my page

BED FOR THE NIGHT WITH SU TUNG-P'O (1036–1101)

I'm resting on the ground
From
My breast the water flows
Where

Does the fountain spring in the stones

Hope is senseless
As is despair
Will no one drink? the bedsheet demands
'Let the rest of your life ebb away . . .'

If I've too much sweat
I've too little ink
More tears than blood
To describe the world
Until I run dry—

THE EMPIRE CONSIDERS A MAP OF THE WORLD

after Zehentmayr's cartoon

America (North) is huge
Coalition of the willing swinging at its hip
Great Britain Italy Spain
And Israel the Colt
Japan becalmed off California

The other continent
Gondwanaland
Takes in Africa Latin-America
Not forgetting Antarctica

A little clump of states far off
With miserable climates
France Belgium Germany Cuba:
Next military objective

Opulent Taiwan
Next door the little island of China
Looks like it might rise up out of the sea

And that oil slick, a crafty touch,
Saudi Iraq Iran
Very interesting

And sketched in at the corner of the map
Russia gone rotten
Inspectors on their way
Staging area for the butchers of Baghdad,
Whose nerves are shot
At the prospect of the liberation of aforementioned China.

ULTIMATUM FOR PARSLEY ISLAND

A few phrases dictated
To this defenceless island . . . What are these traces
Salt and undefined feet
Thickets, breathing, impenetrable.
Cliff tops not accorded to any power.
And swarms of fishes changing sides.
What is there in the interior? Deserts? Commotion
Signs of life (the inspectors will discover them).
These naked hidden gestures, slumbering oil
Unregulated conditions. Is no one here in charge of the sea:
Filth and stubbornness, the separatism of your feelings.
Patrols pick up sinking ships.
What do they whisper, a secret, YAKUZA, JACUZZI
That demands reprisals.
These agile thoughts that turn on the simplest thing.
A coast belonging to no one . . . And anyway
How does it come to lie here in the strident sea.
An independent fleck of white. Surrender little island,
Shake off your refugees, your scrawny goats,
Recognize the new order
Tear up your parsley
And welcome the cataphracts.

THE CENTRE

Then I headed for the centre of the
World. I took a taxi; it lay close by,
A flattened heap of rubble rose before us.
History passed this way on purpose, put the
Boot in and we see desert. The driver
Jostled through the jam, halting
At a shop. Shopping, he said.
Gawping through the door and I saw zilch:
The splendour of the founding years, my century
But not the centre of the world. Me, stubbornly:
To the obelisk.—No shopping? he was
Yelling and beat his brow. I stayed put.
They no longer know where the centre is
Though I have the goal in sight
The place the gods once dwelled, all nine of them,
The Central Committee of Ancient Egypt
And the human spirit communed
With power. The muezzins started
Calling everyone to prayer. I've no clue
Why I was so taken by this place
THE NOTHING THAT WAS SOMETHING THAT
    WILL BE NOTHING
That I could see without looking up
Among the sand that flew right through me.
Shopping, I said quietly.
He gestured me out, pushed off to his prayers
In the middle of the desert of New Cairo
And I went to mine.

HERE'S TO THE GOOD TIMES! FOR SIR PHILIP SIDNEY

Take hold of love for it will pass.
Don't wrench your mind in search of higher things.
Grow rich on life's very transience
Only that which fades, true pleasure brings.

The greater good—forget it, mate:
I get my kicks in the here and now.
Don't be surprised when your backside sags:
What walks the earth, sir, will eat it too.

DE VITA BEATA. AFTER JAIME GIL DE BIEDMA

In an old and clapped-out land
Something like this re-disunited Germany
In a little shithole by the sea
No house of my own and no reserves
Just a heap of memories. Not working
Nor voting, and always paying the bills
And living on without purpose at the cost of the state
Like some precious creature born of most exquisite
    doctrine!

HIDDEN

It's not much cop, this life, to tell the truth
And I observe the strictest codes of dress
For just one slip in my efforts to impress
Would give the lie to how I burn beneath.
If it's a sham I know my flush is bust
And don't I daily reinvent the world?
She's lying on the bed, stark naked, sprawled.
But I'm left on the outside with my lust
Buttoned up like that picture by Courbet,
And ice-bound, voilà—it's Château de Blonay.

(Paris, Musée d'Orsay)

They've lain in the darkness of that chamber
In their long embrace, under the earth,
For five thousand years; so love endures.
(It was the paper told us of their fate:)
Their teeth intact, and scarcely worn away
By that kiss, in which they still persist.
Their lips, though, gnawed away by worms
And nothing left to tell their sex apart.
Are they damned? Beatified by lust
Or was adultery a crime for Stone Age
Man. The world has never happened on a pair
So fallen from the flesh yet holding to the other—
They had no truck with heaven or with hell.
On that night we chose to read no more

MY FEAR

When will I lose my desire? It's what I fear, life
Gone and you fields and lakes, all nature razed.
When I've no love left and no shudder pricks my memory
Summer was hot; the leaves rust away in August.

UNTIMELY

As I lay dozing at my mother's breast
And let the best days of my life go past—
Did I know then I'd sleep through all the rest—

So I was careless—each day as it came;
And as for work? I saw it as a game
And love was nothing but a distant dream:

When was the last time anything entered my head?
Have I spent my whole life living as if I were dead?
Now like a little kid I'm bundled off to bed.

EVERWHERE THE LIGHTS ARE GOING OUT

For Charles Simic

Don't let the people know that day is coming.
Their columns will take over the morning light
Fix knives and chisels, start up the machines
Release the wires and the hidden entrails.

The dossers rise from their cardboard beds disguised
As dustmen, peer inside the empty factories
And pocket the blowtorches that are left behind
Before dispatching three shifts into the abyss.

The days no longer turn to rust, in shreds
The paper that says nothing anyway, the people,
This great oaf, will be good for sweet FA
And less than that, it holds the scrap of hope aloft.

They stand in silence in the darkness
In deep snow in their Sunday dress.
Black-clad, where are they bound? They're bound
Calmly for work where none's now to be found.
In every mitt, tight held, there is a light
So that they will not want for it in the night.
They make an orderly ascension
To church, to the great mouth of St Ann.
'They were all comrades', let go
They climb to the service and say their prayers now.
Their bums get cold on the pews in God's workhouse.
How warm it was in their earth-heated workplace!
They are united as at the face and pray
Bare-headed but it's not God's word they say.
Their supreme being lives in the song about
The foreman coming towards them with his light.

Now it cuts deep. Now it cuts to the core.
The world's going home and *I can't take any more.*
Where's our courage now? Our moment to stand tall?
You moved en masse, let your spirits roam
Became *das Volk.* Now Volker is the name
And I'm to hone my wit upon our fall
And keep my distance in the shopping mall.
We'd like to think that everything will change
Blood, soul and tears for the minimum wage.
Our lives were part and parcel of the deal
What have we become, what can we be?
A race of beggars. Insult to my injury.

IGUANAS

They idle here amongst the grey remains
Of ruined temples, languid, undismayed.
From time to time the flicker of an eye!
Stone-grey the body and rough as stone,
But swift the legs and with a sudden bound
It's back to business, snapping at a fly.

We the iguanas, creatures of a coming age,
Camped in the crumbling citadels of finance
We watch the banks collapse in total silence.
Not the slightest laughter, not a hint of rage.
And power, time? They rot and fall away
And the sun just rises on another day.

> *A Wilderness of sweets; for Nature here*
> *Wantond as in her prime, and plaid at will*
> *Her Virgin Fancies, pouring forth more sweet,*
> *Wilde above Rule or Art; enormous bliss.*

Milton, *Paradise Lost*, Book 5, ll. 294–7

1 *Supper out of skulls*

Like water buffalos my verses scatter
Stubborn words, 'idiotic herds'
I coax them, beat them with twigs and sticks
Images that we don't dare spell out
In the rainy season by a sunken ford
Until one word
                    leaps into the swell
                                    in despair
And the strophe follows without a backward glance
('Cattle, buffalo, smuggled over the border')
At a river between Burma and Thailand

'We took the kiff and the bones marched of their own accord'
... they split the skulls with a sword and ate the brain

Years went by, I was silent
                         fragments
Words hanging on the barbed-wire fence
'picked up', 'interrogated',
                         words on walkabout
Before my closed lips

Under that sun that slits its veins
Something like hunger, like fear (I don't know what it is)
At night the canal of the port of Fiumicino
A match flares in the eyes' hearth
The epic, without name,

                      that sets it off again.

2 *The morning of migrants*

Cádiz, the innards of the rubber dinghy
Abandoned on the sand, I
Stone on the shore have been informed
By the gossiping water.

                      In the great mixer
Of summer the naked and the masked
Who is who, in the carnival of cultures

Where are these folk headed, where will they end up and
     go down?
You cold rubbish-strewn shores of this waning moon.
Where is the solid ground, the warm earth, that the soles
Of their feet can call their home,

                    heels and toes
And the body puts one foot in front of the other effortlessly

They clamber up the cliff face over the stones
Over me and trample on my head
As though it were the goal, a coastline, some kind of sense.
The day strikes them

               down, with its decrees
It blots out their shadows on the *calle mayor*

It leads them towards their destiny

                              with a line of chalk.
They look at me, their oceanic souls
Turned towards the karst of my eyes
Cadaver, cadaver, rolled up into
The crashing plane of the breakers.

3 *Twitter-storm*

Dug-in in your dugout in the summertime
The sandy path is your address, trails of dust hoist
Like flags in the blackbird air,

                              'a refuge for the senses'
The running water, brushwood & fields
From the computer surveillance on the Cyclades /
In the bombing zone Baghdad, a scent of mint
The sweet food of the seasons

I am withered like an olive tree cut down.
Digital idiot with an electronic tag
The twitter-storm erupts, the media cloud
Facts fucked fictions ignite in a flash
Our access to reality slashed and burnt
Societies, wildernesses, impenetrable
Prehistory,

            'post-heroic' (: bad credit risk)

Pound in the hospital garden of Saint Elizabeth's, Washington
Put his verse in the wound

                    usura, usury
That's when profiteering was in its infancy

And *Geldkrieg* I was still to come.
Corporations aren't people and money isn't speech.
There's scuffles in our parliaments, and I've still
To exchange the currency of words, large for small
And your change,

                     hush money.

4 *Wilderness*

You emerge from the womb, anointed with shit,
Alive to the sensations of roaring blood
The beating of the dark lagoon, the secret thread
Connecting this spit, senses primed. You

                            cannot be

closer
To the heart than this, party to unashamed desire
Swimming afraid secure, in the sea of the womb.

Driven out, naked

                 traumatized in the cosmos
Of your own isolation: can you forget your provenance
Your hopes, that safe harbour, brim with amniotic fluid?
Wretched spawn, now you lap at the puddle of

                           Avgas fuel

At Cape Town Airport. I show you a spot

For weddings. Off the beaten track, concealed
Under the blanket of the dunes, salt and grass
At the mouth of the Touws River, Eden District
Where the oceans meet and mix and everything

Is licked back by the

        spray

            to its mineral core.
Oh protean, myriad, wilderness of wholeness
Not folded into any certainty, 'unchecked'
No law tells it how to survive
And I sense once again the desire
Togetherness,

       the necessary, without force
Unrestrained freedom.

5 *Tired of being the material of power*

Sleepwalking along the grand avenues down to the Seine
The gold background of our utopias

         (: there at the PRINTEMPS)
That was your little run before the Wall, clochard
Clutching Ostmarks. Other creatures are also dying out
Man on the march, etc., this species
Set in motion, sweeping over the small-fry . . .

        Continuez!
There's nothing to see here, this accident, MARKETSHOCK
Talked

      to death in the Collège de France. Clear out
Your cave, Encyclop with your round Google-eye
And transform yourself

        according to the new line

           into a barbarian

At base camp, Puerta del Sol . . . The woman demonstrating
Collapsed in a heap on the pavement, 'how tired I am'

(As I said before), and this hazy

                  moment triggered

The whole conspiracy of understanding

At the ground zero of outrage. You hang about

In the reference library

                  of the unhoused (Zhuangzi . . . !)

In between folding beds and clothes racks, the sofas

Madrid mamita mia,

                  of the enraged citizens

                        seized

By the precariat. The sleep-in of the reason of monsters

A standing army all at sea, the Spanish Sea.

6 *Utøya Utopia*

Four Scandiwegians (Norway? Sweden?) on the Underground

Unearthly beauties, their lithe young bodies sway

With the momentum as they hang on the straps, you drink

It in intoxicated,

                  without even wiping your eyes, three

Stations ('of happiness'), and then they vanish

For good at Schönhauser Allee

The pastures of faded love

Craters of flowers, demented feelings.

                        Indifference

You queen of the night. Frisson ploughed back in

Seed and sweat eaten. The chaos inside after reading

The files now put to rest, an Indian elephant

Is what you are, crawled away into the scrub.

                        And the longing

That splits the ground

                          The killing spree on the island edge
Psychologically deregulated, as can only happen to a country
With 'an inner reservoir of unhappiness' and enough ammunition
: *so no one will ever forget me—*
                          I take the weapon
Breivik, it is empty, all the bullets spent, and with this
The massacre is finished, the killings done, the brutality
Well and truly
                  at an end, here in Utøya, for some shoreline of reason,
I dictate an embrace
As overwhelming, as absurd, as a new war.

7 Canto of Traumas

Words like bodies flying
                          from the walls
Of the Twin Towers, words like *action*, death
Freely chosen on the screen with a head for heights
The sentence
                  construction crumples
                                    in on itself in the rubble
Of Manhattan. Random words like bombing raids
By the USA

And sitting there shat upon from
                                    a great height, in Castle Brunnenburg
Him or me, after this or any other World War
Fishing for words in the residual light of blindness
Bookkeeper or novelist of extinction

He glues his arse and his art to the chair
Words like soap, like ashes, the smell of gas
Filthy words, loyalty trust and cod-liver oil
Never to breathe
                    freely again

Or driven by the traffic in the stinking bay at
Eleusis,
              olive trees and mysteries, built-up
Overrun by refineries. These little trees, the cults
Have put paid to work, Denegris writes:
Cold-blooded triumph. Ravaged words like
Work of man or just plain man. Oh God Demeter.
The corn burns in the motors.—Step on it, idiot

8 *Shadow economy*

A brilliant bird-cry zig-zagged yellow into the grey
After the night of rain
                              ripped us from our bed, and we stood
Naked in the chilly dawn, this pocket of air, global
Breathed towards us, foam blossoming white, sloes
Dripping wet, and we
                    took courage
                              at the delivery counter
LA VIE. The fields round Lübars, moor-meandering gaze
Of communism: nature
                              shows us its abundance
From each according to his abilities / To each according to his needs
With its insistent proposition
                              (an election deceit)

Haze of cloud! And the shadow economy of the woods
The plump grass, the plankton revolt to come
'See how the ranks of the millions':

                         mackerel und krill

You must leave this
Earth of mine standing
Without edict or attack of *any meaning*, my hotspot
Is hand-made, you said; a few more (cranial nerve)-
Tracts you must rehearse, mankind, in evolution,
Than Mother Nature dictates. And there we were again
Lying on the white sheet
L'ébauche (*the beginning*), *débouché* (*the mouth*):

                              your body

9 *A saturated satyr*

A saturated satyr
                    resting on his hooves
In front of the supermarket, lusting
After an existence in human form
'Alone in that / gulley . . . one afternoon . . . in history'

What is there left to
                       know, of the stupidity of the world
The horrors are embodied, your bread tastes of guilt
Baked with ash, your pastures
A vat of experience, preserved in vinegar.

Earthquake in the chest cavity, laughter garbage
Hartz 4 Mines 5 towns called misery and woe

Germany! / The state is not me
You surely don't believe that you can let that pass

There is something still left on the table, death
Freshly prepared, 'wholesome'
On the way to a
                        most squalid
                                        fiction!

This little hand that rests in
Yours, sweetness of the moment . . . now follow posterity
In your fastened sack
                        hopping just like that.

To hold in a single thought
Reality and justice.
                        'Leave an old man in peace.'

10 *Universe of Atlantis*

Bathing in marble, feasting on fish guts
I a travelling *Tui* baking in my sun-plunger
My under-spirit soars over a century:
The fruits mouldering vestibules flooded.
The part-time pass-time on the rubble-site
Only sand
            still books
                        the junior suites

Desire, not hope! departs the natural resources
We sink in grid-square references, at home

In Legoland in media,
                              staunch our longing for decay
With everything we can buy, 'fate' (i.e. do nothing).
Finding love for what is to come, supreme art.
I say it here, and as I say it
It is more than I know

The bride on the beach in her pregnant white dress
That's the way the wind is blowing, it's high time
The man pig-headed takes her by the hand
She writes the 'I do' in the sand—

The Tarantula nebula, nursery of the stars: there it is
In the Large Magellanic Cloud
In the constellation of Dorado, an answer for all the world
And out of the entrails
                              of material
                                            they extract the building block
Higgs Boson, in the proton-collider
Goddamn particle, the godless particle.

FINDINGS

For Karen Leeder

My body's wasting away, it cannot tell me why
The sternum juts from underneath the ribs, a hook
On which some gentle breast might fasten for a while
And quicken my blood; as though this were its final berth.
My soul, it too, has shrunken from itself
Force-fed on garbage. Can I bring it through and how.
One lovely thing, it knows, would quench its thirst
Set before it gently; sate it with a glance.

GLUT

Summer burns. The branches break with the weight of apples.
The worm's in every core and is kicked aside.
The world's foot crosses the fields in the morning
And your life and body are scuppered in the bushes.
What's your goal? No goal. Then tell me what grounds you have.
I'm drowning in them. Like mud filling up my mouth.

THE SLUM-DWELLERS OF MEDELLIN TAKE
POSSESSION OF THE GREAT ESCALATOR
27 DECEMBER 2011

I hear that in the infamous city of Medellin
Where immeasurable poverty spreads for miles like a sore
In Communa 13, a no-go area
The Mayor built a gigantic escalator, it cost around seven
    million dollars
So that the pedestrian tribe up there
In the thin air
Might be spared the effort of climbing the steps. For those
    high-born 12,000
On their precipitous stinking slope whose name is Hell
A carpet of imperishable steel has been rolled out
Up the garbage heap
To their jumbled habitations. So technological progress
Reaches them in their zone of want that flour and milk will
    not enter
And where even the light lays only its shadow, but this
Giant stairway climbs like a mountain stream, a vein of silver
To the wretched. I see them

Stepping cautiously onto the treads
In silence, firmly planted, amazed
That without a word this iron ladder
So easy on their feet is at their disposal
And powered by whatever magic
It sets their light bodies in motion between the bare
Brick walls above the corrugated-iron roofs weighted down
With stones. And before they know it
With a thousand untaken steps in a deathly stillness

As though held up for show on the self-propelled conveyor
They arrive without sweating or breathlessness
Dizzyingly twenty-eight storeys high
Or from there quick as cats
Are borne from the edge into the centre. What a lifting

Out of the filth! Such a simple day
Seems here beginning. Minutes without despair
Moments without murder. The discarded
Are taken up and conveyed
Between worlds, between hell and heaven. Returned
So to speak, into civilization, drawn back
Into the great circulation. The primordial solution
Never yet seen in any city: to join incompatibles.
What inventions have to be made, what construction works
Over the rocky back of oppression
Lifts, escape hatches, to lower the level of misery
Fantastic uprisings, castings down
Of all injustice!

EXEQUIES

They wash the dead man in white wine and lay
Him on a bier in the clothes he kept for Sunday
And all his village comes and nips the wine.
Next thing they slit his shirt and trousers open
Which is a sight more laughable than sad.
His body fritters in the wind and sun.
And not a coffin roughly of his size
Enfolds him, only a cloth, he lies
In pumice stone and not beneath the sod
So in a few weeks he has rotted clean.
Only three feet down and still less elbow room
He parks his frame all folded up
And even now he has not come to stop.
In a few years' time they break into this tomb
Salvage his bare bones out of it and then
Rub them over with white wine again.
Like things newborn or lobsters we boil red!
And in the shining casket, going to dust,
In the archive of the graveyard wall they rest.

CONVERSATION ABOUT THE TREES
IN GEZI PARK

1

At issue are a few trees
Silent upright creatures like us
That's to say ordinary, not well-known, easy to clear
From their traditional spot
Where they gather the light in their leaves
A green blaze in the burning heat of cement
Their warm cope the tenement of afternoons.

2

We are talking about trees, alive
And wretched, cut down
In a minor massacre one morning
Like us, an armada of masts going under
In water, wilfulness and teargas
A statistic of happiness that scatters no seed
A season cleared and irrevocable.

3

About trees, then—and a man stops in his tracks
As though he had suddenly seen his muddled feet
As though he were mulling over his lonely gait
He plants himself
On the sodden ground, as though
He were filling his shadow with tangible substance
Sediment of crowds, that evaporates away.

4

As though his own existence
Came to mind, a hasty, stumbling thing
The lack of sleep, of patience
Of something elemental, at root of it all.
It is the trees that remind him
Of the monstrous nature
Of the races and religions gone to the dogs
The subordination of his every breath, the stifling
Of his ability to be human!

5

And the dreamy calculations,
The deficits, the acceptance, the unmade day.
The naked Alps of the future
Billions spent on the water-holes of Arabia, but
The water-cannons have access to secret hydrants.
Coursing over the wretched masses across the seas!

6

The man standing quietly on the street
Is not beyond the reach of injustice.
Endlessly weary, for an endless
Time he stands, gifted
With milk and lemons to wash his eyes:
A forest grows out of his soul,
What times are these, where
A conversation about trees includes all our misdeeds.

DEMON

I'm governed by a curious spirit
Joys it brings and sadness too
I know I can't be cured of it
There's nothing anyone can do.
All my freedom, my constraint,
Arise from this duress.
See how I endure my fate
And suffer my success.

These are the notes included by Volker Braun in the German editions of his poems, along with a few further references of use for English-language readers.

'The Gründel', p. 4

A wooded river-valley in a rural part of Saxony, near Dresden.

'Oysters', p. 10

Importing living creatures into the GDR involved a great deal of paperwork (l. 3). The Wolfs are the writers Gerhard Wolf and his wife, Christa (1929–2011).

'Is It Too Soon. Is It Too Late', p. 11

Thomas Müntzer (c.1489–1525) was a leading German Reformer during the Protestant Reformation, an apocalyptic preacher and a participant in the abortive Peasants' Revolt in Thuringia in 1524–25. Modern Marxists have viewed him as a leader in an early bourgeois revolution against feudalism and the struggle for a classless society. The poem quotes from a letter of 1522 urging the German people to seize the day, and from Martin Luther's famous response.

'Italian Night', p. 14

'TORINO, GRANDE TORINO', etc., were the headlines in the *Gazetta del Populo* on 17 May 1977. The shroud of Jesus is still on display in the Duomo di San Giovanni Battista, Piazza San Giovanni, in Turin.

'Fief', p. 16

The quotation comes from the famous 'Parteilied' written by poet and committed communist Louis Fürnberg (1909–57). Braun's 'fief' also refers back to a poem by the mediaeval German poet Walter von der Vogelweide, 'ich han min lehen'.

'Innermost Africa', p. 17

'*Oh that is where . . .*' and '*Where the lemon trees . . .*' , from Goethe's 'Mignon' poem (1783); 'En quelque soir . . .' and 'Non! We shan't spend another summer . . .' from Rimbaud's *Illuminations* ('Soir historique' and 'Ouvriers', c.1873); '*come, friend, into the open*' and 'For it is not anything vast . . . ' from Hölderlin's unfinished elegy 'Der Gang aufs Land. An Landauer' (1800).

'Daydream', p. 20

'The peoples were silent slumbered . . .' comes from a fragmentary hymn by Friedrich Hölderlin, '1797–98', and many of the formulations refer to Hölderlin. Brecht also appears in the reference to the car stuck between two options: his 'Beim Radwechsel'.

'Walter Benjamin in the Pyrenees', p. 21

The quotation (l. 13) comes from Walter Benjamin's *Arcades Project*, on which he worked from 1927 until his death in 1940, as do many unmarked references in the poem. See also Lisa Fittko's account of Benjamin's final journey across the Pyrenees: *Escape through the Pyrenees* (1991). The Spanish is quoted from the death register at Portbou, which lists a black briefcase with 'papers of unknown content' among the effects of the deceased. Neither was recovered.

'Dark Places', p. 23

To be precise, Hölderlin says: 'But alas, our kind walks in darkness it dwells as in Orcus, / Severed from all that's divine. To his own industry only/ Each man is forged, and can hear only himself in his workshop's / Deafening noise; and much the savages toil there, for ever / Moving their powerful arms, they labour, yet always and always / Vain, like the Furies, unfruitful the wretches' exertions remain there' ('The Archipelago', 1800).

Hans K. Koch, literary critic and Party functionary, died in 1986.

Anton Günther (1836–1937), perhaps the best known local poet and folk singer from the Erzgebirge region. His dialect song 'Es ist Feierabend' is still popular today.

'Another Part of the Heath', p. 27

The line 'This is a night: to cool a courtezan' appears in Shakespeare's *King Lear*, 3.2.

'Gallery of Antiquities', p. 29

'The man living next door to the runway': a metaphor from Rudolf Bahro's lecture 'Who Can Stop the Apocalypse?' (1982). 'Durchgearbeitete Landschaft' (Worked-Through Landscape) is the title of one of Braun's well-known earlier poems (1974) about the industrial exploitation of the earth. 'Listen to see if your heart is still beating': graffiti in Spiegelgasse, Zurich. 'Cordula I love you! Nicolette', and 'Civilisaturation': graffiti in Basel. 'Zuvielisation'—a mixture of civilisation and 'zu viel' (excess)—is now a recognized word in German in a way it is not (yet) in English.

'The Zig-Zag Bridge', p. 32

The so-called nine-bend bridge in the Yuyuan Garden in Shanghai, which led to the private garden of the governor Pan Yunduan and was supposedly impassable for evil spirits. To the politically exhausted traveller of May 1988, the bridge was a metaphor for history 'good / for surprises', in expectation of the changes of 1989.

'Prologue for the Opening of the Fortieth Season of the Berliner Ensemble on 11 October 1989', p. 39

The wagon is that of the trader *Mother Courage* in Brecht's play of 1939 about the Thirty Years War, where it symbolizes the fetishism of trade above all else. The 'iron truck' appears as a representation of socialism in a number of poems and in Braun's play *Lenins Tod* (written in 1970, first published in 1988).

'O Chicago! O Contradiction!', p. 45

The poem answers Brecht's famous poem 'Vom armen B.B.' (1927).

'Property', p. 46

The poem responds to the older text 'Fief' (1980) in which the question was posed: 'How will I survive the frozen structures'. It also cites an article by the West German journalist Ulrich Greiner, in *Die Zeit*, 22 July 1990, which lambasted East German intellectuals for their naive idealism, entitled 'Die toten Seelen des Realsozialismus sollen bleiben wo der Pfeffer wächst' (The dead souls of really existing socialism can go to hell).

'9 November', p. 47

'BERLIN /NUN FREUE DICH' 'BERLIN/ REJOICE', said by Bürgermeister Momper the night the Wall was breached.

'Theatre of the Dead', p. 49

Rotoli: near Palermo; the graveyard has the form of an amphi-theatre. Jupiter's forearm from the ruins of Thuburbo Majus can be seen in the Bardo museum. Friedrich Schorlemmer, the Wittenberg Protestant theologian active in the Civil Rights movement in the GDR, called his fellow East Germans 'Privatpöbel' (a phrase borrowed from Marx for the politically disinterested): 'of service to whoever feeds their faces with something good'.

'Marlboro Is Red. Red Is Marlboro', p. 52

The answer of Philip Morris' 'marketing philosophy depart-ment' to the question they posed themselves: 'What is red?'

'Balance', p. 62

The Gaukbehörde in Normannenstraße, Berlin, is where after 1990 an archive of secret police files from the GDR was kept under the directorship of Pastor Joachim Gauck. These were made available to victims of surveillance for consultation.

'Pliny sends Greetings to Tacitus', p. 63

Pliny the Younger reports the death of his uncle, Pliny the Elder, during the eruption of Vesuvius in 79 CE in his *Epistles*.

'The Magma in the Heart of the Tuareg', p. 65

The penultimate line derives from Rimbaud's *Illuminations* ('Vagabonds') *c*.1873.

'6. 5. 1996', p. 66

A. R. Penck, the painter from Dresden. Theo Adam and Peter Schreier (singers), Ludwig Güttler (trumpeter), Rolf Hoppe (actor) and later Friedrich Goldmann (composer): all well known in the GDR and members of the Saxon Academy of Arts.

King Kurt is Kurt Biedenkopf, *Ministerpräsident* of Saxony. 'TRUE, IF THE CHILDREN . . . ' is from Brecht's poem 'Die Jugend im Dritten Reich' (the lines continue 'Then we could go on telling them fairy stories'). 'When will the poet be born . . . ' derives from Diderot's *Dissertation sur le poème dramatique* (1758).

'Hill of the Dead', p. 69

The Tumulus of Tumiac at the Gulf of Morbihan, Brittany. 'The astonishing land breeze', from Braun's poem 'The Turning Point', 1988.

'Bay of the Dead', p. 70

After a Breton legend about the Baie des Trépassés. For Hans Mayer.

'After the Massacre of Illusions', p. 72

'FOLLOW YOUR FINE PHRASES' is said by Deputy Mercier to his fellow prisoners in Act III of Georg Büchner's play *Dantons Tod* (1835). Danton replies: 'Nowadays they do everything in human flesh . . . They will use my body too'.

'Lagerfeld', p. 73

Was written in 1997 and is the epilogue to Braun's play *Limes. Mark Aurel* (2002). It quotes from Heinrich von Kleist's letter to his cousin Marie on 19 November 1811, two days before he committed suicide.

'Dances of Death', p. 77

'Dances of death: not the estates but the state of things, with distorted concepts. It is the dance of society'. Braun's note to this cycle depends on a pun ('Stände'/'Zustände').

It was Walter Benjamin, in his *Arcades* project and elsewhere, who claimed 'The concept of progress should be based on catastrophe. That things "just keep on going" is the catastrophe.' Braun's modern 'danse macabre' cites Brecht's 'Keiner oder alle', set to music by Hanns Eisler in 1934, with its chorus: 'Everything or nothing. All of us or none'; and varies Brecht's 'Solidaritätslied' also set by Eisler: 'Vorwärts und nicht vergessen' (Forwards *without* forgetting). The *Communist Manifesto* states: 'The history of all hitherto existing society is the history of class struggles'. 'WE KNOW WE CAN'T HOLD ON TO ANYTHING' is a response to a line in Hölderlin's late poem 'Mnemosyne' (1803) which charts the battle to hold on to memory ('Vieles ist aber zu behalten'; A lot wants keeping).

'Berlin-Mitte', p. 89

The Dorotheenstadt Cemetery in the Mitte area of Berlin houses the graves of Hegel, Fichte, Brecht, Anna Seghers, Christa Wolf, Heiner Müller and the poet Karl Mickel.

'Tides', p. 90

The East German worker-hero Adolf Hennecke famously increased the work–production norms by 274 per cent in a single night, but was apparently motivated, not by ambition, nor socialist commitment, but by his insatiable hunger. The quotation 'And fresh sustenance new blood / I suck from the free world' is from Goethe's poem 'Auf dem See' of 1775.

'Shakespeare Shuttle', p. 92

'The Happy Unemployed' was originally a manifesto written by unemployed Berliners in the summer of 1996. Within a few months, an informal network of the 'Happy Unemployed' had sprung up across Germany, publishing a magazine and carrying out ironic interventions against the enforcement of back-to-work schemes.

Grigori Michailowitsch Kosinzew was a Russian filmmaker and theatre director who found fame with his work on Shakespeare. Mosfilm is the largest Russian film studio.

'Women on Waves' was a Dutch initiative to provide family-planning services on a ship in international waters for women in countries where such services are illegal.

'The Empire Considers a Map of the World', p. 98

Dieter Zehentmayr was an Austrian cartoonist (1943–2005). The cartoon 'The New Order' appeared on 2 April 2003.

'Ultimatum for Parsley Island', p. 99

This uninhabited, rocky islet (less than half a square mile) is located in the southern shore of the Strait of Gibraltar, some 250 metres from the Moroccan coast. Its sovereignty is disputed between Spain and Morocco and was the subject of a military incident between the two countries in 2002.

'Here's to the Good Times! For Sir Philip Sidney', p. 101

For in 1585 Sir Philip Sidney *bade a long farewell to glittering pleasures* ('Splendidis longum valedico nugis').

'De vita beata. After Jaime Gil de Biedma', p. 102

The Spanish poet Jaime Gil de Biedma's poem of the same title is a vision of Spain 'between two civil wars'.

'Hidden', p. 103

Gustav Courbet's painting 'L'origine du monde' of 1866 was for many years hidden behind a winter landscape depicting the Château de Blonay.

'The Last-Shift Mass', p. 108

Traditionally, a mass and a celebration held at night after the ending of the last shift before Christmas. Here: such an event after the closure of the mine.

'Cashing Up', p. 109

This poem, published in 2009, forms a trio with 'Fief' (1980) and 'Property' (1990). It quotes the poem 'Er beklagt die Enderung und Furchtsamkeit itziger Deutschen' (He laments the lack of steadfastness and timidity of present-day Germans) by Paul Fleming (1609–40). Volker, as well as being a pun on the inflationary tendency of the famous *Wende* phrase 'Wir sind das Volk' and the poet's own name, refers to the hero and artist figure Volker in the *Niebelungen* saga.

'Wilderness', p. 111

1.

A match flares in the eyes' hearth is quoted from Ezra Pound's *Cantos* (1915–62) and is one of a number of references to Pound in the poem. Some of the later place names (Castle Blumenberg, St Elizabeth's Hospital) also refer to stations in Pound's life.

Under that sun that slits its veins comes from Pier Paolo Pasolini's poem 'A Desperate Vitality' from *Poesia in forma di rosa* (1964).

3.

'Corporations aren't people and money isn't speech' refers to the US Supreme Court's controversial ruling on the campaign-finance reform case *Citizens United v. FEC* of 2010.

5.

'Madrid du Wunderbare' ('Madrid you wonderful') here rendered with another phrase from the same song, 'Mamita mia', comes from Ernst Busch's Spanish Civil War song 'Los Cuatro Generales'.

The square Puerta del Sol, Madrid, is one of the key focus points of a Spanish protest movement (known as the 15-M Movement or Indignants' Movement) which has organized many events since 2011 against unemployment and the European sovereign debt crisis.

6.

On 2 July 2012, the right-wing fanatic Anders Breivik detonated a bomb in Oslo killing 8 and then went on a killing spree at a Workers' Youth League Camp on the island of Utøya, off the coast of Norway, killing 69—mainly young people. The quotation is his.

7.

The Eleusinian Mysteries were initiation ceremonies held every year for the cult of Demeter and Persephone based at Eleusis in ancient Greece.

8.

'From each according to his ability, to each according to his need' is a slogan popularized by Karl Marx in his 1875 *Critique of the Gotha Programme*, and looks forward to a time of abundance in a socialist society where everyone's needs will be fulfilled.

'See how the ranks of the millions' comes from the song 'Brüder zur Sonne zur Freiheit' which originated in a prison in tsarist Russia in the nineteenth century and was taken over by the Workers' Movement and later in the GDR.

9.

Hartz 4 Mines 5: the original phrase 'Hartz 4 Brocken 5' is untranslatable. It refers to the introduction of the Hartz IV initiative in Germany in 2005, the central plank of 'Agenda 2010', a sweeping set of social reforms that would become Chancellor Gerhard Schroeder's legacy. It subsumed social welfare benefits into the unemployment benefit system and pegged both at the lower level of former social assistance, sparking protests across the country and a rift in the Social Democratic Party. The Brocken is a mountain in the Harz region of Germany, which also appears in Goethe's *Faust*. The phrase 'ein harter Brocken' means a bitter pill, or something hard to swallow. 'Sorge' and 'Elend', the two place names mentioned in the same line, are small towns in the Harz with telling names (literally: 'sorrow' and 'misery').

'To hold in a single thought reality and justice' is quoted from W. B. Yeats' revised version of *A Vision* (1937), which was dedicated to Ezra Pound and also contained 'A Packet for Ezra Pound' on *The Cantos*.

10.

Bertolt Brecht coined the term 'Tui' (formed from the acronym of a pun on the word 'intellectual') for an intellectual who sells his or her abilities or opinions as a commodity in the market place to support the dominant ideology. He coined it in the mid-1930s and used it in a range of material including his *Turandot, or the Whitewashers' Congress* (1953–54).

The Higgs Boson, also known as the God particle, is an elementary particle first theorized in 1964 and finally discovered at the Large Hadron Collider at CERN in July 2012.

'The Slum-Dwellers of Medellin Take Possession of the Great Escalator 27 December 2011', p. 124

See Brecht's 'Inbesitznahme der grossen Metro durch die Moskauer Arbeiterschaft am 27. April 1935'.

'Conversation about the Trees in Gezi Park', p. 127

Taksim Gezi Park is a small urban park next to Taksim Square in Istanbul. The Turkish protester Erdem Gunduz was dubbed the 'standing man' when he led a vigil on Taksim Square in 2013, days after the authorities evicted demonstrators. See Brecht's famous poem 'An die Nachgeborenen', written in exile from fascism in 1938, where 'a conversation about trees is almost a crime / because it implies silence about so many misdeeds'.

'The Gründel' ('Das Gründel', 1959, Karen Leeder trans.), 'Demand' ('Anspruch', 1962, Karen Leeder trans.) in *Provokation für mich* (Halle: Mitteldeutscher Verlag, 1965).

'An Account of Despair' ('Bericht von der Verzweiflung', 1969, David Constantine trans.), 'The Life and Times of Volker Braun' ('Der Lebenswandel Volker Brauns', 1971, Karen Leeder trans.), 'Oysters' ('Die Austern', 1973, David Constantine trans.) in *Gegen die symmetrische Welt* (Halle: Mitteldeutscher Verlag, 1974).

'Is It Too Soon. Is It Too Late' ('Ist es zu früh. Ist es zu spät', 1974, Karen Leeder trans.), 'Afternoon' ('Der Mittag', 1975, Karen Leeder trans.), 'Definition' ('Definition', 1975, Karen Leeder trans.), 'Italian Night' ('Italienische Nacht', 1976, Karen Leeder trans.), 'Prussia, Pleasure Garden' ('Lustgarten, Preußen', 1977, Karen Leeder trans.) in *Training des aufrechten Gangs* (Halle: Mitteldeutscher Verlag, 1979).

'Fief' ('Das Lehen', 1980, Karen Leeder trans.), 'Innermost Africa' ('Das innerste Afrika', 1982, David Constantine trans.), 'Daydream' ('Tagtraum', 1986, Karen Leeder trans.) in *Langsamer knirschender Morgen* (Frankfurt am Main: Suhrkamp Verlag, 1987).

'Walter Benjamin in the Pyrenees' ('Benjamin in den Pyrenäen', 1986, Karen Leeder trans.), 'Dark Places' ('Die dunklen Orte', 1986, Karen Leeder trans.), 'Woken out of Dogmatic Slumber' ('Aus dem dogmatischen Schlummer geweckt', 1987, David Constantine trans.), 'Breakfast' ('Das Frühstück', 1987, David Constantine trans.), 'Another Part of the Heath' ('Andere

Gegend auf der Heide', 1987, Karen Leeder trans.), 'Gallery of Antiquities' ('Antikensaal', 1988, Karen Leeder trans.) in *Der Stoff zum Leben 1–3* (Frankfurt am Main: Suhrkamp Verlag, 1992).

'The Zig-Zag Bridge' ('Die Zickzackbrücke', 1988, David Constantine trans.), 'The Turning Point' ('Die Wende', 1988, David Constantine trans.), 'The Cinnamon Forest' ('Der Zimtwald', 1988, David Constantine trans.), 'The Muddy Levels' ('Die Schlammebene', 1988, David Constantine trans.), 'Builder on the Stalinallee' ('Der Maurer von der Stalinallee', 1988, David Constantine trans.), 'New Wallpaper' ('Tapetenwechsel', 1988, David Constantine trans.), 'The Colony' ('Die Kolonie', 1989, Karen Leeder trans.), 'Prologue for the Opening of the Fortieth Season of the Berliner Ensemble on 11 October 1989' ('Prolog zur Eröffnung der 40. Spielzeit des Berliner Ensembles am 11. Oktober 1989', 1989, Karen Leeder trans.), 'O Chicago! O Contradiction!' ('O Chicago! O Widerspruch!', 1990, Karen Leeder trans.), 'Property' ('Das Eigentum', 1990, Karen Leeder trans.), '9 November' ('Der 9. November', 1990, David Constantine trans.), 'Ambra' ('Ambra', 1991, David Constantine trans.), 'My Brother' ('Mein Bruder', 1991, David Constantine trans.), 'Marlboro Is Red. Red Is Marlboro' ('Marlboro ist red. Red ist Marlboro', 1991, David Constantine trans.), 'Theatre of the Dead' ('Das Theater der Toten', 1991, Karen Leeder trans.), 'End of October in August' ('Ende Oktober im August', 1991, Karen Leeder trans.), in *Die Zickzackbrücke: Ein Abrißkalender* (Halle: Mitteldeutscher Verlag, 1992).

'Rubble Flora' ('Die Trümmerflora', 1963, David Constantine trans.), 'At Dawn', ('Die Morgendämmerung', 1971, Karen Leeder trans.) in *Texte in zeitlicher Folge*, VOL. 3 (1993).

'West Shore' ('Der Weststrand', 1995, David Constantine trans.) (Warmbronn: Verlag Ulrich Keicher, 1995).

'Pliny Sends Greetings to Tacitus' ('Plinius grüsst Tacitus', 1996, David Constantine trans.), 'The Magma in the Heart of the Tuareg' ('Das Magma in der Brust des Tuareg', 1996, David Constantine trans.), '6. 5. 1996' ('6. 5. 1996', 1996, David Constantine trans.), 'Hill of the Dead' ('Der Totenhügel', 1993, Karen Leeder trans.), 'The Bay of the Dead' ('Die Bucht der Hingeschiedenen', 1996, Karen Leeder trans.), 'After the Massacre of Illusions' ('Nach dem Massaker der Illusionen', 1997, David Constantine trans.), 'Lagerfeld' ('Lagerfeld', 1997, David Constantine trans.) in *Tumulus* (Frankfurt am Main: Suhrkamp Verlag, 1999).

'Utopia' ('Die Utopie', 2000, Karen Leeder trans.), 'Communism' ('Der Kommunismus', 2000, Karen Leeder trans.), 'Common Ownership' ('Das Volkseigentum', 2000, Karen Leeder trans.), 'Ideology' ('Die Ideologie', 2000, Karen Leeder trans.), 'Class Struggle' ('Der Klassenkampf', 2000, Karen Leeder trans.), 'Solidarity' ('Die Solidarität', 2000, Karen Leeder trans.), 'Art' ('Die Kunst', 2000, David Constantine trans.) in *Neue Totentänze. Holzstiche von Karl-Georg Hirsch. Mit Gedichten von Volker Braun, Peter Gosse, Kerstin Hensel, Richard Pietraß, Hubert Schirneck und Kathrin Schmidt* (Hubert Kästner ed.) (Frankfurt am Main: Insel Verlag, 2002).

'Balance' ('Das Gleichgewicht', 1993, Karen Leeder trans.), 'Coined for the Ruling Class' ('Gemünzt auf die herrschende Klasse', 2000, Karen Leeder trans.), 'Pontine Marshes' ('Pontinische Sümpfe', 2001, Karen Leeder trans.), 'Paradiso' ('Paradiso', 2001, Karen Leeder trans.), 'Berlin-Mitte' ('Berlin-Mitte', 2001, Karen Leeder trans.), 'Shakespeare Shuttle' ('Shakespeare-Shuttle', 2001, Karen Leeder trans.), 'World Power' ('Die Weltmacht', 2002, Karen Leeder trans.), 'Bed for the Night with Su Tung-P'o (1036–1101)' ('Gelage, nachts, mit Su Dung-Po', 2002, Karen Leeder trans.), 'Tides' ('Die Gezeiten', 1988/2002, Karen Leeder trans.), 'Here's to the

Good Times! For Sir Philip Sydney' ('Auf die schönen Possen! An Sir Philip Sydney', 2003, Karen Leeder trans.), 'De vita beata. After Jaime Gil de Biedma' ('De vita beata. Nach Jaime Gil de Biedma', 2003, Karen Leeder trans.), 'Ultimatum for Parsley Island' ('Ultimatum an die Petersilieninsel', 2003, Karen Leeder trans.), 'My Fear' ('Meine Furcht', 2003, Karen Leeder trans.), 'The Empire Considers a Map of the World' ('Das Imperium schaut auf die Weltkarte', 2003, Karen Leeder trans.), 'The Centre' ('Der Mittelpunkt', 2004, Karen Leeder trans.), 'When He Could See Again' ('Als er wieder sehen konnte', 2004, Karen Leeder trans.) in *Auf die schönen Possen* (Frankfurt am Main: Suhrkamp Verlag, 2005).

Poems up to 1991 appeared also in Volker Braun, *Texte in zeitlicher Folge*, 10 VOLS (Halle: Mitteldeutscher Verlag, 1989–93). A substantial selection, from which much of this selection is taken, appeared in *Lustgarten, Preußen: Ausgewählte Gedichte* (Frankfurt am Main: Suhrkamp Verlag, 2000).

'Untimely' ('Die Unzeit', 2006, Karen Leeder trans.), 'Everywhere the Lights Are Going Out' ('Überall gehn die Lampen aus', 2006, Karen Leeder trans.), 'Iguanas' ('Die Leguane', 2007, Karen Leeder trans.), 'The Lovers. Before Dante' ('Die Liebenden. Vor Dante', 2007, Karen Leeder trans.), 'Hidden' ('Der Verborgene', 2008, Karen Leeder trans.), 'Cashing Up' ('Kassensturz', 2009, Karen Leeder trans.), 'The Last-Shift Mass' ('Die Mettenschicht', 2010, David Constantine trans.), 'Wilderness' ('Wilderness', 2012, Karen Leeder trans.), 'Findings' ('Die Befunde', 2012, Karen Leeder trans.), 'Glut' ('Der Überfluß', 2012, Karen Leeder trans.), 'The Slum Dwellers of Medellin Take Possession of the Great Escalator 27 December 2011' ('Inbesitznahme der großen Rolltreppe durch die Medelliner Slumbewohner am 27. Dezember 2011', 2012, David Constantine trans.), 'Exequies' ('Totenfeier', 2012, David Constantine trans.), 'Demon'

('Dämon', 2012, Karen Leeder trans.), 'Conversation about the Trees in Gezi Park' ('Gespräch über die Bäume im Gezi-Park', 2013, Karen Leeder trans.) uncollected.